After the Last Sky

After the Last Sky

Palestinian Lives

EDWARD W. SAID

PHOTOGRAPHS BY

JEAN MOHR

faber and faber

LONDON · BOSTON

First published in 1986
by Faber and Faber Limited
3 Queen Square London WC1N 3AU

Printed in Great Britain by
Butler and Tanner Ltd Frome Somerset

British Library Cataloguing in Publication Data
Said, Edward W.
After the last sky.
1. Palestinian Arabs – Social conditions
I. Title II. Mohr, Jean
305.8'9275694 DS113.7

ISBN 0-571-13683-4

Contents

Acknowledgments

The writing of this book owes a great deal to several people whose help, encouragement, and interest were invaluable. In London Donald Mitchell of Faber and Faber, in New York André Schiffrin of Pantheon, gave us early signs of solidarity and backing. Later, Sara Bershtel's painstaking and sensitive editorial surveillance polished and sharpened the manuscript. Deborah Poole, my assistant at Columbia, worked on the text, especially in its relationship with the photographs, with precision and insight. Various close friends – Deirdre and Alan Bergson, Julie Diamond and Eqbal Ahmad, Janet and Ibrahim Abu-Lughod, Richard Poirier – gave me informed and refined readings. To Kamal Boulatta, Ibrahim Dakkak, Tania and Hanna Nasir, Mirène Ghossein, Fran Anteman, Noubar Hovsepian, Elie Sanbar, Shafik al-Hout, and Mahmoud Darwish (whose poetry has illuminated almost every part of the Palestinian experience, and one of whose lines I borrowed as this book's title), I owe thanks for suggestions and favors too various to detail. Mariam Said watched over our efforts with her characteristic wit and loving support.

E.W.S.

New York, 1986

Where should we go after the last frontiers,
where should the birds fly after the last sky?
                                    Mahmoud Darwish

INTRODUCTION # Palestinian Lives

The idea of this book grew out of the peculiar circumstances that first brought Jean Mohr and me together. In 1983, while I was serving as a consultant to the United Nations for its International Conference on the Question of Palestine (ICQP), I suggested that photographs of Palestinians be hung in the entrance hall to the main conference site in Geneva. I had of course known and admired Mohr's work with John Berger, and I recommended that he be commissioned to photograph some of the principal locales of Palestinian life. Given the initial enthusiasm for the idea, Mohr left on a special U.N.-sponsored trip to the Near East. The photographs he brought back were indeed wonderful; the official response, however, was puzzling and, to someone with a taste for irony, exquisite. You can hang them up, we were told, but no writing can be displayed with them. No legends, no explanations. A compromise was finally negotiated whereby the name of the country or place (Jordan, Syria, Lebanon, West Bank, Gaza) could be affixed to the much-enlarged photographs, but not one word more. When Jean and I met it was this strange and inflexible formula that we confronted.

As with all bureaucratic organizations, we got only bureaucratic explanations for the prohibition on writing, and I must say that I cannot remember any of them. What I do remember with certainty, however, is that the opposition was ascribed to 'some U.N. member states,' who during all the preparatory phases of the ICQP had found any sustained writing on the Palestinian people objectionable and difficult in principle to accept. These member states, alas, were principally Arab, and their various problems with even the idea of ICQP make for a sorry and disgraceful record. Palestine to them was useful up to a point – for attacking Israel, for railing against Zionism, imperialism, and the United States, for bewailing the settlement and expropriation of Arab land in the Occupied Territories. Beyond that point, when it came to the urgent needs of the Palestinians *as a people,* or to the deplorable conditions in which many Palestinians live in Arab countries as well as in Israel, lines had to be drawn. During the year preceding the conference I had commissioned at least twenty studies, all of them mandated by the General Assembly, designed to provide the participants in ICQP – exclusively governments – with requisite information on our people. Only three papers survived to become official documents of the conference. The others were cut down and rejected because one after another Arab state objected to this or that principle, this or that insinuation, this or that putative injury to its sovereignty. Israel and the United States did not deign to take note of any aspect of ICQP.

It was then that Jean Mohr and I decided to work together. Let us use photographs and a text, we said to each other, to say something that hasn't been said about Palestinians. Yet the problem of writing about and representing – in all senses of the word – Palestinians in some fresh way is part of a much larger problem. For it is not as if no one speaks about or portrays the Palestinians. The difficulty is that everyone, including the Palestinians themselves, speaks a very great deal. A huge body of literature has grown up, most of it polemical, accusatory, denunciatory. At this point, no one writing about Palestine – and indeed, no one going to Palestine – starts from scratch: We have all been there before, whether by reading about it, experiencing its millenial presence and power, or actually living there for periods of time. It is a terribly crowded place, almost too crowded for what it is asked to bear by way of history or interpretation of history.

Yet, for all the writing about them, Palestinians remain virtually unknown. Especially in the West, particularly in the United States, Palestinians are not so much a people as a pretext for a call to arms. It is certainly correct to say that we are less known than our co-claimants to Palestine, the Jews. Since 1948, our existence has been a lesser one. We have experienced a great deal that has not been recorded. Many of us have been killed, many permanently scarred and silenced, without a trace. And the images used to represent us only diminish our reality further. To most people Palestinians are visible principally as fighters, terrorists, and lawless pariahs. Say the word 'terror' and a man wearing a *kaffiyah* and mask and carrying a *kalachnikov* immediately leaps before one's eyes. To a degree, the image of a helpless, miserable-looking refugee has been replaced by this menacing one as the veritable icon of 'Palestinian.'

In the meantime, the enormous changes in the situation of the Palestinians continue to complicate our reality, almost daily. In one season some of us are massacred at Sabra and Shatila by Lebanese Maronite militiamen acting under Israeli direction (it is important to dot *i*'s and cross *t*'s, to be clear about who is responsible); in another season it is the Amal Shi'ite militia, probably acting under the orders of Syria, that besieges the same camps of Sabra and Shatila and

4

commits many of the same atrocities that only a short time before had become the horrific symbols of Israeli brutality.

Among Palestinians today, an increasingly urgent subject of discussion arises whenever we gather: the way in which we are treated, whether by Arab friends or Israeli enemies. Sometimes it is not easy to say where and by whom the treatment is worse. Although every Palestinian knows perfectly well that what has happened to us for the last three decades is a direct consequence of Israel's destruction of our society in 1948, the question – both political and perceptual – remains whether a clear, direct line can be drawn from our misfortunes in 1948 to our misfortunes in the present.

I don't think that such a line can be drawn; no clear and simple narrative is adequate to the complexity of our experience. Even if it is true that Israel has relentlessly pursued us both inside and outside the Arab world, fighting Palestinian nationalism and even the idea of Palestine without quarter since 1948, our experiences in the Arab states are *Arab* experiences after all, and they stand on their own. Wherever we are, we are dogged by our past, but we have also created new realities and relationships that neither fit simple categories nor conform to previously encountered forms.

There are yet other complexities. The one thing that none of us can forget is that violence has been an extraordinarily important aspect of our lives. Whether it has been the violence of our uprooting and the destruction of our society in 1948, the violence visited on us by our enemies, the violence we have visited on others, or, most horribly, the violence we have wreaked on each other – these dimensions of the Palestinian experience have brought us a great deal of attention, and have exacerbated our self-awareness as a community set apart from others. While many of us would say immediately that we have suffered more violence than we have caused others to suffer, that everything we have done has been in self-defense, and that there is an implicit agreement among Arab, Israeli, and U.S. governments to do away with us as a political force, most of us would concede also that the dynamics of Palestinian life, at least since 1967, have developed a particular logic that does not admit of so simple and reductive an apologetic. Yes, we have been victimized and our identity has been threatened, but no, we have been neither passive nor innocent. The passions provoked by us, in other words, testify to a considerable independent power of our own, which it would be bad faith to deny.

To be sure, no single Palestinian can be said to feel what most other Palestinians feel: Ours has been too various and scattered a fate for that sort of correspondence. But there is no doubt that we do in fact form a community, if at heart a community built on suffering and exile. How, though, to convey it? The thing about our exile is

5

that much of it is invisible and entirely special to us. We are at once too recently formed and too variously experienced to be a population of articulate exiles with a completely systematic vision, and too voluble and troublemaking to be simply a pathetic mass of refugees. 'Palestinians,' an older relative has been saying to me for at least twenty-five years, 'are a sickness.' I don't share his view, although the fact that we fall between a number of classifications undoubtedly causes our friends, our enemies, and ourselves a lot of difficulties; certainly it contributes to the problem of writing about and representing the Palestinians generally.

The whole point of this book is to engage this difficulty, to deny the habitually simple, even harmful representations of Palestinians, and to replace them with something more capable of capturing the complex reality of their experience. Its style and method – the interplay of text and photos, the mixture of genres, modes, styles – do not tell a consecutive story, nor do they constitute a political essay. Since the main features of our present existence are dispossession, dispersion, and yet also a kind of power incommensurate with our stateless exile, I believe that essentially unconventional, hybrid, and fragmentary forms of expression should be used to represent us. What I have quite consciously designed, then, is an alternative mode of expression to the one usually encountered in the media, in works of social science, in popular fiction. It is a personal rendering of the Palestinians as a dispersed national community – acting, acted upon, proud, tender, miserable, funny, indomitable, ironic, paranoid, defensive, assertive, attractive, compelling.

This is not an 'objective' book. Our intention was to show Palestinians through Palestinian eyes without minimizing the extent to which even to themselves they feel different, or 'other.' Many Palestinian friends who saw Jean Mohr's pictures thought that he saw us as no one else has. But we also felt that he saw us as we would have seen ourselves – at once inside and outside our world. The same double vision informs my text. As I wrote, I found myself switching pronouns, from 'we' to 'you' to 'they,' to designate Palestinians. As abrupt as these shifts are, I feel they reproduce the way 'we' experience ourselves, the way 'you' sense that others look at you, the way, in your solitude, you feel the distance between where 'you' are and where 'they' are.

The multifaceted vision is essential to any representation of us. Stateless, dispossessed, de-centered, we are frequently unable either to speak the 'truth' of our experience or to make it heard. We do not usually control the images that represent us; we have been confined to spaces designed to reduce or stunt us; and we have often been distorted by pressures and powers that have been too much for us. An additional problem is that our language, Arabic, is unfamiliar in the West and belongs to a tradition and civilization usually both misunderstood and maligned. Everything we write about ourselves, therefore, is an interpretive translation – of our language, our experience, our senses of self and others.

But it is only through a recognition of these complexities that we can approach the elusive nature of identity, or integrate public and private realities, or apprehend that extraordinary variety of individuals and activities called Palestinian. And just as Jean Mohr and I, a Swiss and a Palestinian, collaborated in the process, we would like you – Palestinians, Europeans, Americans, Africans, Latin Americans, Asians – to do so also.

E.W.S.
New York, 1986

Photographer's note

Passing through New York about two years ago, I visited a photographer friend, a respected reporter and a perfect connoisseur of the world of photography. After a cordial exchange of news, impressions and memories, he asked me the ritual question:

'And what projects are you working on at the moment?'

'An exhibition, showing the result of thirty years of reporting and publications, and also some rather more aesthetic experiments, in color. At the same time, I'm working on the completion of a new book, something very close to my heart.'

'What's it about?'

'The Palestinians.'

There was rather a long silence, then my friend looked at me with a slightly sad smile, and said, eventually:

'Sure, why not! But don't you think the subject's a bit *dated*? Look, I've taken photographs of Palestinians too, especially in the refugee camps . . . it's really sad! But these days, who's interested in people who eat off the ground with their hands? And then there's all that terrorism . . . I'd have thought you'd be better off using your energy and capabilities on something more worthwhile!'

It is precisely in response to this kind of foolishness that I have persevered with the project of this book. But I must explain briefly the motivation behind my interest in the Palestinian cause. Some facts and dates will serve as a guide.

1925 I was born in Geneva of German nationality; both my parents originally came from South Germany.

1936 Request for Swiss naturalization for the whole family – the word 'exile' ceases to be an abstract idea.

1939 I become a Swiss citizen.

1949 The International Red Cross Committee takes me on as a delegate, and I am sent to the Middle East as part of a team acting on behalf of Palestinian refugees. Having recently graduated from the University of Geneva, I know practically nothing about the situation there – but I am full of good intentions and determined to show myself up to the task. After three months in the general area of Beirut, off to Jericho, then Hebron. Food distribution, setting up camps and schools, taking a census.

1950 Red Cross Aid is coming to an end; I go on working for a few months as 'area officer' in Irbed, with the U.N.

1967 Two-week trip to Israel and the West Bank.

1979 I am offered the chance to make a one-month tour of Israel and the Occupied Territories (West Bank), accompanied by a friend who speaks Hebrew and Arabic equally well: it's a traumatic experience! Thirty years on, the situation of the Palestinians, far from improving, has deteriorated even more. In the camps, the tents have been replaced by huts in which the refugees freeze in winter and suffocate in summer. A new generation is born: but with what future, what hope?

The Israelis are not solely to blame, we are all guilty. Myself too for having tried to forget the fate of the Palestinians for thirty years with the fallacious excuse that the outrages carried out by the most extreme among them were in no case justifiable.

Of the pictures I brought back from there, some have been published, but always in small-circulation periodicals, and in a context I would willingly describe as academic. An intellectual readership, then, and with a bias towards the left (or liberal, as the Americans say), in other words, readers already half-convinced of the justification of Palestinian claims.

I then returned several times to the Middle East: to Lebanon, Syria, Jordan, specifically to visit the camps.

At the end of my last stay in Israel, just before setting off to Switzerland from Tel Aviv airport, the customs officer, a young and amiable Sabra, asked some questions which I found thoroughly indiscreet:

'Have you enjoyed your stay in our country? Where did you stay? . . . and did you see any Arabs?'

'Listen, unless you keep your eyes closed it's difficult not to see Arabs in Israel!'

'I'm sorry, I meant: did you visit any Arabs?'

She was confused; I did not insist. I gave her a smile and headed on to the embarkation gate. Yes, I had visited some Arabs, and some Israelis too, but this was neither the time nor the place to explain, or to attempt to persuade.

Jean Mohr
Geneva, June 1985

Tripoli, Badawi camp, May 1983.

1 States

Caught in a meager, anonymous space outside a drab Arab city, outside a refugee camp, outside the crushing time of one disaster after another, a wedding party stands, surprised, sad, slightly uncomfortable. Palestinians – the telltale mixture of styles and attitudes is so evidently theirs – near Tripoli in northern Lebanon. A few months after this picture was taken their camp was ravaged by intra-Palestinian fighting. Cutting across the wedding party's path here is the ever-present Mercedes, emblazoned with its extra mark of authenticity, the proud *D* for *Deutschland*. A rare luxury in the West, the Mercedes – usually secondhand and smuggled in – is the commonest of cars in the Levant. It has become what horse, mule, and camel were, and then much more. Universal taxi, it is a symbol of modern technology domesticated, of the intrusion of the West into traditional life, of illicit trade. More important, the Mercedes is the all-purpose conveyance, something one uses for everything – funerals, weddings, births, proud display, leaving home, coming home, fixing, stealing, reselling, running away in, hiding in. But because Palestinians have no state of their own to shield them, the Mercedes, its provenance and destination obscure, seems like an intruder, a delegate of the forces that both dislocate and hem them in. 'The earth is closing on us, pushing us through the last passage,' writes the poet Mahmoud Darwish.

The paradox of mobility and insecurity. Wherever we Palestinians are, we are not in our Palestine, which no longer exists. You travel, from one end of the Arab world to the other, in Europe, Africa, the Americas, Australia, and there you find Palestinians like yourself who, like yourself, are subject to special laws, a special status, the markings of a force and violence not yours. Exiles at home as well as abroad, Palestinians also still inhabit the territory of former Palestine (Israel, the West Bank, Gaza), in sadly reduced circumstances. They are either 'the Arabs of Judea and Samaria,' or, in Israel, 'non-Jews.' Some are referred to as 'present absentees.' In

Arab countries, except for Jordan, they are given special cards identifying them as 'Palestinian refugees,' and even where they are respectable engineers, teachers, business people, or technicians, they know that in the eyes of their host country they will always be aliens. Inevitably, photographs of Palestinians today include this fact and make it visible.

Memory adds to the unrelieved intensity of Palestinian exile. Palestine is central to the cultures of Islam, Christianity, and Judaism; Orient and Occident have turned it into a legend. There is no forgetting it, no way of overlooking it. The world news is often full of what has happened in Palestine-Israel, the latest Middle East crisis, the most recent Palestinian exploits. The sights, wares, and monuments of Palestine are the objects of commerce, war, pilgrimage, cults, the subjects of literature, art, song, fantasy. East and West, their high and their commercial cultures, have descended on Palestine. Bride and groom wear the ill-fitting nuptial costumes of Europe, yet behind and around them are the clothes and objects of their native land, natural to their friends and attendants. The happiness of the occasion is at odds with their lot as refugees with nowhere to go. The children playing nearby contrast starkly with the unappealing surroundings; the new husband's large workman's hands clash with his wife's delicate, obscuring white. When we cross from Palestine into other territories, even if we find ourselves decently in new places, the old ones loom behind us as tangible and unreal as reproduced memory or absent causes for our present state.

Sometimes the poignancy of resettlement stands out like bold script imposed on faint pencil traces. The fit between body and new setting is not good. The angles are wrong. Lines supposed to decorate a wall instead form an imperfectly assembled box in which we have been put. We perch on chairs uncertain whether to address or evade our interlocutor. This child is held out, and yet also held in. Men and women re-express the unattractiveness around them: The angle made across her face by the woman's robe duplicates the ghastly wall pattern, the man's crossed feet repeat and contradict the outward thrust of the chair leg. He seems unsettled, poised for departure. Now what? Now where? All at once it is our transience and impermanence that our visibility expresses, for we can be seen as figures forced to push on to another house, village, or region. Just as we once were taken from one 'habitat' to a new one, we can be moved again.

Exile is a series of portraits without names, without contexts. Images that are largely unexplained, nameless, mute. I look at them without precise anecdotal knowledge, but their realistic exactness nevertheless makes a deeper impression than mere information. I cannot reach the actual people who were photographed, except through a European photographer who saw them for me. And I

Tel Sheva, 1979. A village of settled nomads near Bersheeba. Some years ago, these people still lived in a tent, under the desert sky. The carpet on the ground is the only reminder of that earlier period.

imagine that he, in turn, spoke to them through an interpreter. The one thing I know for sure, however, is that they treated him politely but as someone who came from, or perhaps acted at the direction of, those who put them where they so miserably are. There was the embarrassment of people uncertain why they were being looked at and recorded. Powerless to stop it.

·····

When A. Z.'s father was dying, he called his children, one of whom is married to my sister, into his room for a last family gathering. A frail, very old man from Haifa, he had spent his last thirty-four years in Beirut in a state of agitated disbelief at the loss of his house and property. Now he murmured to his children the final faltering words of a penniless, helpless patriarch. 'Hold on to the keys and the deed,' he told them, pointing to a battered suitcase near his bed, a repository of the family estate salvaged from Palestine when Haifa's Arabs were expelled. These intimate mementos of a past irrevocably lost circulate among us, like the genealogies and fables of a wandering singer of tales. Photographs, dresses, objects severed from their original locale, the rituals of speech and custom: Much reproduced, enlarged, thematized, embroidered, and passed around, they are strands in the web of affiliations we Palestinians use to tie ourselves to our identity and to each other.

Sometimes these objects, heavy with memory – albums, rosary beads, shawls, little boxes – seem to me like encumbrances. We carry them about, hang them up on every new set of walls we shelter in, reflect lovingly on them. Then we do not notice the bitterness, but it continues and grows nonetheless. Nor do we acknowledge the frozen immobility of our attitudes. In the end the past owns us. My father spent his life trying to escape these objects, 'Jerusalem' chief among them – the actual place as much as its reproduced and manufactured self. Born in Jerusalem, as were his parents, grandparents, and all his family back in time to a distant vanishing point, he was a child of the Old City who traded with tourists in bits of the true cross and crowns of thorn. Yet he hated the place; for him, he often said, it meant death. Little of it remained with him except a fragmentary story or two, an odd coin or medal, one photograph of his father on horseback, and two small rugs. I never even saw a picture of my grandmother's face. But as he grew older, he reverted to old Jerusalemite expressions that I did not understand, never having heard them during the years of my youth.

Amman, 1984. A visit to the former mayor of Jerusalem and his wife, in exile in Jordan.

·····

Ramallah, 1979.
An everyday street scene,
banal and reassuring. And
yet, the tension is constant.
A passing military jeep, a
flying stone – the incident,
the drama, can occur at
any moment.

Identity – who we are, where we come from, what we are – is difficult to maintain in exile. Most other people take their identity for granted. Not the Palestinian, who is required to show proofs of identity more or less constantly. It is not only that we are regarded as terrorists, but that our existence as native Arab inhabitants of Palestine, with primordial rights there (and not elsewhere), is either denied or challenged. And there is more. Such as it is, our existence is linked negatively to encomiums about Israel's democracy,

16

achievements, excitement; in much Western rhetoric we have slipped into the place occupied by Nazis and anti-Semites; collectively, we can aspire to little except political anonymity and resettlement; we are known for no actual achievement, no characteristic worthy of esteem, except the effrontery of disrupting Middle East peace. Some Israeli settlers on the West Bank say: 'The Palestinians can stay here, with no rights, as resident aliens.' Other Israelis are less kind. We have no known Einsteins, no Chagall, no Freud or Rubinstein to protect us with a legacy of glorious achievements. We have had no Holocaust to protect us with the world's compassion. We are 'other,' and opposite, a flaw in the geometry of resettlement and exodus. Silence and discretion veil the hurt, slow the body searches, soothe the sting of loss.

··········

A zone of recollected pleasure surrounds the few unchanged spots of Palestinian life in Palestine. The foodsellers and peddlers – itinerant vendors of cakes or corn – are still there for the casual eye to see, and they still provoke the appetite. They seem to travel not only from place to place, but from an earlier time to the present, carrying with them the same clientele – the young girls and boys, the homeward-bound cyclist, the loitering student or clerk – now as then. We buy their wares with the same surreptitiously found change (who can remember the unit? was it a piaster? fils? shilling?) spent on the same meager object, neither especially good nor especially well prepared. The luxurious pleasure of tasting the

vendor's *simsim,* the round sesame cakes dipped in that tangy mixture of thyme and sumac, or his *durra,* boiled corn sprayed with salt, surpasses the mere act of eating and opens before us the altogether agreeable taste of food not connected with meals, with nourishment, with routine. But what a distance now actually separates me from the concreteness of that life. How easily traveled the photographs make it seem, and how possible to suspend the barriers keeping me from the scenes they portray.

For the land is further away than it has ever been. Born in Jerusalem in late 1935, I left mandatory Palestine permanently at the end of 1947. In the spring of 1948, my last cousin evacuated our family's house in West Jerusalem; Martin Buber subsequently lived there till his death, I have been told. I grew up in Egypt, then came to the United States as a student. In 1966 I visited Ramallah, part of the Jordanian West Bank, for a family wedding. My father, who was to die five years later, accompanied my sister and me. Since our visit, all the members of my family have resettled – in Jordan, in Lebanon, in the United States, and in Europe. As far as I know, I have no relatives who still live in what was once Palestine. Wars, revolutions, civil struggles have changed the countries I have lived in – Lebanon, Jordan, Egypt – beyond recognition. Until thirty-five years ago I could travel from Cairo to Beirut overland, through territories held or in other ways controlled by rival colonial powers. Now, although my mother lives in Beirut, I have not visited her since the Israeli invasion of 1982: Palestinians are no longer welcome there. The fact is that today I can neither return to the places of my youth, nor voyage freely in the countries and places that mean the most to me, nor feel safe from arrest or violence even in the countries I used to frequent but whose governments and policies have changed radically in recent times. There is little that is more unpleasant for me these days than the customs and police check upon entering an Arab country.

Consider the tremendous upheavals since 1948, each of which effectively destroyed the ecology of our previous existence. When I was born, we in Palestine felt ourselves to be part of a small community, presided over by the majority community and one or another of the outside powers holding sway over the territory. My family and I, for example, were members of a tiny Protestant group within a much larger Greek Orthodox Christian minority, within the larger Sunni Islam majority; the important outside power was Britain, with its great rival France a close second. But then after World War II Britain and France lost their hold, and for the first time we directly confronted the colonial legacy – inept rulers, divided populations, conflicting promises made to resident Arabs and mostly European Jews with incompatible claims. In 1948, Israel was established; Palestine was destroyed, and the great Palestinian dispossession began. In 1956 Egypt was invaded by Britain, France, and Israel, causing what was left of the large Levantine communities there (Italian, Greek, Jewish, Armenian, Syrian) to leave. The rise of Abdel Nasser fired all Arabs – especially Palestinians – with the hope of a revived Arab nationalism, but after the union of Syria with Egypt failed in 1961, the Arab cold war, as it has been called, began in earnest; Saudi Arabia versus Egypt, Jordan versus Syria, Syria versus Iraq. . . . A new population of refugees, migrant workers, and traveling political parties crisscrossed the Arab world. We Palestinians immersed ourselves in the politics of Baathism in Syria and Iraq, of Nasserism in Egypt, of the Arab Nationalist Movement in Lebanon.

The 1967 war was followed shortly after by the Arab oil boom. For the first time, Palestinian nationalism arose as an independent force in the Middle East. Never did our future seem more hopeful. In time, however, our appearance on the political scene stimulated, if it did not actually cause, a great many less healthy phenomena: fundamentalist Islam, Maronite nationalism, Jewish zealotry. The new consumer culture, the computerized economy, further exacerbated the startling disparities in the Arab world between rich and poor, old and new, privileged and disinherited. Then, starting in 1975, the Lebanese civil war pitted the various Lebanese sects, the Palestinians, and a number of Arab and foreign powers against each other. Beirut was destroyed as the intellectual and political nerve center of Arab life; for us, it was the end of our only important, relatively independent center of Palestinian nationalism, with the Palestinian Liberation Organization at its heart. Anwar Sadat recognized Israel, and Camp David further dismantled the region's alliances and disrupted its balance. After the Iranian revolution in 1979 came the Iran-Iraq war. Israel's 1982 invasion of Lebanon put more Palestinians on the move, as the massacres in the Palestinian refugee camps of Sabra and Shatila reduced the community still further. By the end of 1983, Palestinians were fighting each other, and Syria and Libya were directly involved, supporting Palestinian dissidents against PLO loyalists. With the irony typical of our political fate, however, in mid-1985 we were united together in Sabra and Shatila to fight off a hostile Shi'ite militia patronized by Syria.

The stability of geography and the continuity of land – these have completely disappeared from my life and the life of all Palestinians. If we are not stopped at borders, or herded into new camps, or denied reentry and residence, or barred from travel from one place to another, more of our land is taken, our lives are interfered with arbitrarily, our voices are prevented from reaching each other, our identity is confined to frightened little islands in an inhospitable environment of superior military force sanitized by the clinical jargon of pure administration. On the West Bank and in Gaza we confront several Zionist 'master plans' – which, according to Meron Benvenisti, ex-deputy mayor of Jerusalem, are 'explicitly sectarian.' He continues:

> The criteria established to determine priorities of settlement regions are *'interconnection* [*havirah*] between existing Jewish areas for the creation of [Jewish] settlement continuity' and *'separation* [*hayitz*] to restrict uncontrolled Arab settlement and the prevention of Arab settlement blocs'; *'scarcity* [*hesech*] refers to areas devoid of Jewish settlement.' In these criteria 'pure planning and political planning elements are included.'
>
> (*The West Bank Data Project:*
> *A Survey of Israeli Policies*)

Continuity for *them*, the dominant population; discontinuity for *us*, the dispossessed and dispersed.

The circle is completed, though, when we Palestinians acknowledge that much the same thesis is adhered to by Arab and other states where sizable Palestinian communities exist. There too we are in dispersed camps, regions, quarters, zones; but unlike their Israeli counterparts, these places are not the scientific product of 'pure planning' or 'political planning.' The Baqa'a camp in Amman, the Palestinian quarter of Hawaly in Kuwait, are simply there.

All forms of Palestinian activity, all attempts at unity, are suspect. On the West Bank and Gaza, 'development' (the systematic strengthening of Palestinian economic and social life) is forbidden, whereas 'improvement' is tolerated so long as there isn't too much of it; so long as it doesn't become development. The colors of the Palestinian flag are outlawed by Israeli military law; Fathi Gabin of Gaza, an artist, was given a six-month prison sentence for using black, green, red, and white in one of his works. An exhibit of Palestinian culture at al-Najah University in Nablus earned the school a four-month closing. Since our history is forbidden, narratives are rare; the story of origins, of home, of nation is underground. When it appears it is broken, often wayward and meandering in the extreme, always coded, usually in outrageous forms – mock-epics, satires, sardonic parables, absurd rituals – that make little sense to an outsider. Thus Palestinian life is scattered, discontinuous, marked by the artificial and imposed arrangements of interrupted or confined space, by the dislocations and unsynchronized rhythms of disturbed time. Across our children's lives, in the open fields in which they play, lie the ruins of war, of a borrowed or imported industrial technology, of cast-off or abandoned forms. How odd the conjuncture, and yet for Palestinians, how fitting. For where no straight line leads from home to birthplace to school to maturity, all events are accidents, all

Tyre, South Lebanon, 1983. Bourj el-Shemali camp. The car bears witness to a drama, circumstances unknown. The flowers: the month of May, it is spring. The children: wearing smart clothes, almost certainly donated by a charity. They are refugees – the children of refugees.

progress is a digression, all residence is exile. We linger in nondescript places, neither here nor there; we peer through windows without glass, ride conveyances without movement or power. Resourcefulness and receptivity are the attitudes that serve best.

The difference between the new generation of Palestinians and that of 1948 is striking. Our parents bore on their faces the marks of disaster uncomprehended. Suddenly their past had been interrupted, their society obliterated, their existence radically impoverished. Refugees, all of them. Our children know no such past. Cars are equally for riding or, ruined, for playing in. Everything around them seems expendable, impermanent, unstable, especially where – as in Lebanon – Palestinian communities have been disastrously depleted or destroyed, where much of their life is undocumented, where they themselves are uncounted.

No Palestinian census exists. There is no line that can be drawn from one Palestinian to another that does not seem to interfere with the political designs of one or another state. While all of us live among 'normal' people, people with complete lives, they seem to us hopelessly out of reach, with their countries, their familial continuity, their societies intact. How does a Palestinian father tell his son and daughter that Lebanon (Egypt, Syria, Jordan, New York) is where we are, but not where we are *from*? How does a mother confirm her intimate recollections of childhood in Palestine to her children, now that the facts, the places, even the names, are no longer allowed to exist?

· · · · · · · · · · · ·

So we borrow and we patch things together. Palestinians retain the inflections of Jaffa, of Hebron, of Jerusalem and other cities left behind, even as their dialect becomes that of Beirut, Detroit, or Paris. I have found out much more about Palestine and met many more Palestinians than I ever did, or perhaps could have, in pre-1948 Palestine. For a long time I thought that this was so because I was a child then, somewhat sheltered, a member of a minority. But my experience is confirmed by my oldest and closest Palestinian friend, Ibrahim Abu-Lughod. Although he was more in and of pre-1948 Palestine – because older, more conscious and active – than I ever was, he too says that he is much more in contact with Palestinians today than when he was in Palestine. He writes, 'Thanks to modern technological progress, Palestinian families, and Palestinian society as a whole, have been able to forge very numerous human, social, and political links. By getting on a plane I can see the majority of my friends. It's because of this that our family has remained unified. I see all the members of my family at least once or twice a year. Being in Jaffa, I could never have seen relatives who lived in Gaza, for example.' But Ibrahim does not celebrate this sociability: 'I constantly experience the sense that something is missing for me. To compensate for this lack, I multiply and intensify human contacts.'

Over the missing 'something' are superimposed new realities. Plane travel and phone conversations nourish and connect the fortunate; the symbols of a universal pop culture enshroud the vulnerable.

Bedouin encampment near Bersheeba, 1979.

· · · · · · · · · · ·

There can be no orderly sequence of time. You see it in our children who seem to have skipped a phase of growth or, more alarming, achieved an out-of-season maturity in one part of their body or mind while the rest remains childlike. None of us can forget the whispers and occasional proclamations that our children are 'the population factor' – to be feared, and hence to be deported – or constitute special targets for death. I heard it said in Lebanon that Palestinian children in particular should be killed because each of them is a potential terrorist. Kill them before they kill you.

Gaza, 1979.
Refugee camp.
A boy of unknown age.

Tel Sheva, 1979.
A group portrait,
taken at the request of the
children.

25

How rich our mutability, how easily we change (and are changed) from one thing to another, how unstable our place – and all because of the missing foundation of our existence, the lost ground of our origin, the broken link with our land and our past. There are no Palestinians. Who are the Palestinians? 'The inhabitants of Judea and Samaria.' Non-Jews. Terrorists. Troublemakers. DPs. Refugees. Names on a card. Numbers on a list. Praised in speeches – *el pueblo palestino, il popolo palestino, le peuple palestinien* – but treated as interruptions, intermittent presences. Gone from Jordan in 1970, now from Lebanon.

None of these departures and arrivals is clean, definitive. Some of us leave, others stay behind. Remnants, new arrivals, old residents. Two great images encapsulate our unresolved existence. One is the identity card (passport, travel document, laissez-passer), which is never Palestinian but always something else; it is the subject of our national poem, Mahmoud Darwish's 'Bitaqit Hawia': 'Record! I am an Arab/Without a name – without title/patient in a country/with people enraged. And the second is Emil Habiby's invention the Pessoptimist (*al-mutasha 'il*), the protagonist of a disorderly and ingenious work of Kafkaesque fiction, which has become a kind of national epic. The Pessoptimist is being half here, half not here, part historical creature, part mythological invention, hopeful and hopeless, everyone's favorite obsession and scapegoat. Is Habiby's character fiction, or does his extravagant fantasy only begin to approximate the real? Is he a made-up figure or the true essence of our existence? Is Habiby's jamming-together of words – *mutafa'il* and *mutasha'im* into *mutasha'il,* which repeats the Palestinian habit of combining opposites like *la* ('no') and *na'am* ('yes') into *la'am* – a way of obliterating distinctions that do not apply to us, yet must be integrated into our lives?

· · · · · · · ·

Emile Habiby is a craggy, uncompromisingly complex, and fearsomely ironic man from Haifa, son of a Christian family, Communist party stalwart, longtime Knesset member, journalist, editor. His novel about the Pessoptomist (whose first name, incidentally, is Said) is chaotic because it mixes time, characters, and places; fiction, allegory, history, and flat statement, without any thread to guide the reader through its complexities. It is the best work of Palestinian writing yet produced, precisely because the most seemingly disorganized and ironic. In it we encounter characters whose names are of particular significance to Palestinians: The name of Yuaad, the work's female lead, means 'it shall be repeated,' a reference to the string of defeats that mark our

Bersheeba, 1979. Near a Bedouin encampment, a little kitchen garden – and its scarecrow of bits and pieces.

history, and the fatalistic formulae that color our discourse. One of the other characters is Isam al-Bathanjani – Isam the Eggplant, a lawyer who is not very helpful to Said but who keeps turning up just the same. So it is with eggplants in Palestine. My family – my father in particular – has always been attached to eggplants from Battir, and during the many years since any of us had Battiri eggplants the seal of approval on good eggplants was that 'they're almost as good as the Battiris.'

Gaza, 1979. Farm using refugee labor.

Today when I recall the tiresome paeans to Battiris, or when in London and Paris I see the same Jaffa oranges or Gaza vegetables grown in the *bayarat* ('orchards') and fields of my youth, but now marketed by Israeli export companies, the contrast between the inarticulate rich *thereness* of what we once knew and the systematic export of the produce into the hungry mouths of Europe strikes me with its unkind political message. The land and the peasants are bound together through work whose products seem always to have meant something to other people, to have been destined for consumption elsewhere. This observation holds force not just because the Carmel boxes and the carefully wrapped eggplants are emblems of the power that rules the sprawling fertility and enduring human labor of Palestine, but also because the discontinuity between me, out here, and the actuality there is so much more compelling now than my receding memories and experiences of Palestine.

Another, far more unusual, item concerning this vegetable appears in an article by Avigdor Feldman, 'The New Order of the Military Government: State of Israel Against the Eggplant,' which appeared in the journal *Koteret Rashit,* August 24, 1983. Laws 1015 and 1039, Feldman reports, stipulate that any Arab on the West Bank and Gaza who owns land must get written permission from the military governor before planting either a new vegetable – for example, an eggplant – or fruit tree. Failure to get permission risks one the destruction of the tree or vegetable plus one year's imprisonment.

Exile again. The facts of my birth are so distant and strange as to be about someone I've heard of rather than someone I know. Nazareth – my mother's town. Jerusalem – my father's. The pictures I see display the same produce, presented in the same carelessly plentiful way, in the same rough wooden cases. The same people walk by, looking at the same posters and trinkets, concealing the same secrets, searching for the same profits, pleasures, and goals. The same as what? There is little that I can truly remember about Jerusalem and Nazareth, little that is specific, little that has the irreducible durability of tactile, visual, or auditory memories that concede nothing to time, little – and this is the 'same' I referred to – that is not confused with pictures I have seen or scenes I have glimpsed elsewhere in the Arab world.

Palestine is exile, dispossession, the inaccurate memories of one place slipping into vague memories of another, a confused recovery of general wares, passive presences scattered around in the Arab environment. The story of Palestine cannot be told smoothly. Instead, the past, like the present, offers only occurrences and coincidences. Random. The man enters a quiet alley where he will pass cucumbers on his right, tomatoes on his left; a priest walks down the stairs, the boy dashes off, satchel under arm, other boys loiter, shopkeepers look out for business; carrying an airline bag, a man advances past a display of trinkets, a young man disappears around the corner, two boys idle aimlessly. Tomatoes, watermelons, arcades, cucumbers, posters, people, eggplants – not

Nazareth, 1979.
Portrait of Om Kalsoum.

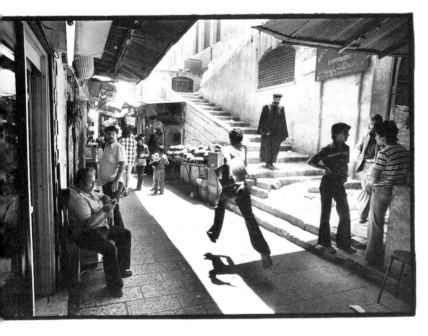

Jerusalem, 1979.
A snapshot.

Jerusalem, 1979.
A snapshot.

simply there, but represented by photographs as being there – saturated with meaning and memory, and still very far away. Look more closely and think through these possibilities: The poster is about Egypt. The trinkets are made in Korea or Hong Kong. The scenes are surveyed, enclosed, and surrounded by Israelis. European and Japanese tourists have more access to Jerusalem and Nazareth than I do. Slowly, our lives – like Palestine itself – dissolve into something else. We can't hold to the center for long.

············

Exile. At a recent conference in America featuring a 'dialogue' between Israeli and Palestinian intellectuals with reconciliation high on the agenda, a man rises from the audience to pose a question. 'I am a Palestinian, a peasant. Look at my hands. I was kicked out in 1948 and went to Lebanon. Then I was driven out, and went to Africa. Then to Europe. Then to here. Today [he pulls out an envelope] I received a paper telling me to leave this country. Would one of you scholars tell me please: Where am I supposed to go now?' No one had anything to tell him. He was an embarrassment, and I have no idea what in fact he did, what became of him. My shame.

The Palestinian's claims on Israel are generally unacknowledged, much less seen as directly connected to the founding of the state. On the Arabs there is an ambivalent Palestinian claim, recognized in Arab countries by countless words, gestures, threats, and promises. Palestine, after all, is the centerpiece of Arab nationalism. No Arab leader since World War II has failed to make Palestine a symbol of his country's nationalist foreign policy. Yet, despite the avowals, we have no way of knowing really how they – all the 'theys' – feel about us. Our history has cost every one of our friends a great deal. It has gone on too long.

Let Ghassan Kanafani's novella *Men in the Sun* stand for the fear we have that unless we press 'them' they will allow us to disappear, and the equal worry that if we press them they will either decry our hectoring presence, and quash it in their states, or turn us into easy symbols of their nationalism. Three refugees concealed in the belly of a tanker truck are being transported illegally across the border into Kuwait. As the driver converses with the guards, the men (Palestinians) die of suffocation – in the sun, forgotten. It is not the driver's forgetfulness that nags at him. It is their silence. 'Why didn't you knock on the sides of the tank? Why didn't you bang the sides of the tank? Why? Why? Why?' Our fear to press.

············

*Old City of Jerusalem,
1984. A tourist shop.
Customers are rare. Will
they be American, Swiss,
or Israeli?*

The Palestinians as commodity. Producing ourselves much as the
masabih, lamps, tapestries, baskets, embroideries, mother-of-pearl
trinkets are produced. We turn ourselves into objects not for sale,
but for scrutiny. People ask us, as if looking into an exhibit case,
'What is it you Palestinians want?' – as if we can put our demands
into a single neat phrase. All of us speak of *awdah*, 'return,' but do
we mean that literally, or do we mean 'we must restore ourselves to
ourselves'? The latter is the real point, I think, although I know
many Palestinians who want their houses and their way of life back,
exactly. But is there any place that fits us, together with our
accumulated memories and experiences?

Jerusalem, 1979.

Do we exist? What proof do we have?

The further we get from the Palestine of our past, the more precarious our status, the more disrupted our being, the more intermittent our presence. When did we become 'a people'? When did we stop being one? Or are we in the process of becoming one? What do those big questions have to do with our intimate relationships with each other and with others? We frequently end our letters with the mottoes 'Palestinian love' or 'Palestinian kisses'. Are there really such things as Palestinian intimacy and embraces, or are they simply intimacy and embraces, experiences common to everyone, neither politically significant nor particular to a nation or a people?

The politics of such a question gets very close to our central dilemma: We all know that we are Arabs, and yet the concept, not to say the lived actuality, of Arabism – once the creed and the discourse of a proud Arab nation, free of imperialism, united, respected, powerful – is fast disappearing, cut up into the cautious defensiveness of relatively provincial Arab states, each with its own traditions – partly invented, partly real – each with its own nationality and restricted identity. In addition, Palestine has been replaced by an Israel whose aggressive sense of itself as the state of the Jewish people fuels the exclusivity of a national identity won and maintained to a great extent at our expense. We are not Jews, we have no place there except as resident aliens, we are outsiders. In

34

the Arab states we are in a different position. There we are Arabs, but it is the process of nationalization that excludes us: Egypt is for and by Egyptians, Iraq is for and by Iraqis, in ways that cannot include Palestinians whose intense national revival is a separate phenomenon. Thus we are the same as other Arabs, and yet different. We cannot exist except as Arabs, even though 'the Arabs' exist otherwise as Lebanese, Jordanians, Moroccans, Kuwaitis, and so forth.

Add to this the problems we have of sustaining ourselves as a collective unit and you then get a sense of how *abstract,* how very solitary and unique, we tend to feel.

Village of Ramah, Galilee, 1979. A secular high school with students from thirty-six neighboring villages.

Strip off the occasional assertiveness and stridency of the Palestinian stance and you may catch sight of a much more fugitive, but ultimately quite beautifully representative and subtle, sense of identity. It speaks in languages not yet fully formed, in settings not completely constituted, like the shy glance of a child holding her father's knee while she curiously and tentatively examines the stranger who photographs her. Her look conjures up the unappreciated fact of birth, that sudden, unprepared-for depositing of a small bundle of self on the fields of the Levant after which comes the trajectory of dispossession, military and political violence, and that constant, mysterious entanglement with monotheistic religion at its most profound – the Christian Incarnation and Resurrection, the Ascension to heaven of the Prophet Mohammed, the Covenant of Yahweh with his people – that is knotted definitively in Jerusalem, center of the world, *locus classicus* of Palestine, Israel, and Paradise.

Amman, 1984. Pediatric clinic.

Sidon, South Lebanon, 1983. A refugee writes out a message destined for her husband, a prisoner in the camp at Ansar.

A secular world of fatigue and miraculously renewed energies, the world of American cigarettes and an unending stream of small papers pulled out of miscellaneous notebooks or 'blocnotes,' written on with disposable pens, messages of things wanted, of people missing, of requests to the bureaucracy. The Palestinian predicament: finding an 'official' place for yourself in a system that makes no allowances for you, which means endlessly improvising solutions for the problem of finding a missing loved one, of planning a trip, of entering a school, on whatever bit of paper is at hand. Constructed and deconstructed, ephemera are what we negotiate with, since we authorize no part of the world and only influence increasingly small bits of it. In any case, we keep going.

The striking thing about Palestinian prose and prose fiction is its formal instability: Our literature in a certain very narrow sense *is* the elusive, resistant reality it tries so often to represent. Most literary critics in Israel and the West focus on what is said in Palestinian writing, who is described, what the plot and contents deliver, their sociological and political meaning. But it is *form* that should be looked at. Particularly in fiction, the struggle to achieve form expresses the writer's efforts to construct a coherent scene, a narrative that might overcome the almost metaphysical impossibility of representing the present. A typical Palestinian work will always be concerned with this peculiar problem, which is at once a problem of plot and an enactment of the writer's enterprise. In Kanafani's *Men in the Sun* much of the action takes place on the dusty streets of an Iraqi town where three Palestinian men must petition, plead, and bargain with 'specialists' to smuggle them across the border into Kuwait. Impelled by exile and dislocation, the Palestinians need to carve a path for themselves in existence, which for them is by no means a given or stable reality. Like the history of the lands they left, their lives seem interrupted just before they could come to maturity and satisfaction; thus each man leaves behind family and responsibilities, to whose exigencies he must answer – unsuccessfully – here in the present. Kanafani's very sentences express instability and fluctuation – the present tense is subject to echoes from the past, verbs of sight give way to verbs of sound or smell, and one sense interweaves with another – in an effort to defend against the harsh present and to protect some particularly cherished fragment of the past. Thus, the precarious actuality of these men in the sun reproduces the precarious status of the writer, each echoing the other.

Our characteristic mode, then, is not a narrative, in which scenes take place *seriatim,* but rather broken narratives, fragmentary compositions, and self-consciously staged testimonials, in which the narrative voice keeps stumbling over itself, its obligations, and its limitations.

· · · · · · · · ·

Each Palestinian structure presents itself as a potential ruin. The theme of the formerly proud family house (village, city, camp) now wrecked, left behind, or owned by someone else, turns up everywhere in our literature and cultural heritage. Each new house is a substitute, supplanted in turn by yet another substitute. The names of these places extend all the way from the private (my friend Mohammed Tarbush expatiates nobly on the beauties of Beit Natif, a village near Bethlehem that was wiped out of existence by Israeli bulldozers in 1948; his widowed mother now lives in Jarash, Jordan,

Sidon, South Lebanon, 1983. Camp at Ein-el-Hilwé. Time passes: destruction, reconstruction, redestruction.

he in Paris) to the official, or institutionalized, sites of ruin – Deir Yassin, Tell el-Zaatar, Birim and Ikrit, Ein el-Hilwé, Sabra, Shatila, and more. Even 'Palestine' itself is such a place and, curiously, already appears as a subject of elegy in journalism, essays, and literature of the early twentieth century. In the works of Halim Nassar, Ezzat Darwaza, Khallil Beidas, and Aref el-Aref, Palestine's destruction is predicted.

All cultures spin out a dialectic of self and other, the subject 'I' who is native, authentic, at home, and the object 'it' or 'you,' who is foreign, perhaps threatening, different, out there. From this dialectic comes the series of heroes and monsters, founding fathers and barbarians, prized masterpieces and despised opponents that express a culture from its deepest sense of national self-identity to its refined patriotism, and finally to its coarse jingoism, xenophobia, and exclusivist bias. For Palestinian culture, the odd thing is that its own identity is more frequently than not perceived as 'other.' 'Palestine' is so charged with significance for others that Palestinians cannot perceive it as intimately theirs without a simultaneous sense of its urgent importance for others as well. 'Ours' but not yet fully 'ours.' Before 1948, Palestine had a central agonistic meaning both for Arab nationalism and for the Zionist movement. After 1948, the parts of Palestine still inhabited by Arabs took on the additional label of the 'non-Jewish' part of the Jewish state. Even a picture of an Arab town – like Nazareth where my mother was born and grew up – may express this alienating perspective. Because it is taken from outside Nazareth (in fact, from Upper Nazareth, a totally Jewish addition to the town, built on the surrounding hills), the photograph renders Palestine as 'other.' I never knew Nazareth, so this is my only image of it, an image of the 'other,' from the 'outside,' Upper Nazareth.

Arab Nazareth, 1979. Viewed from Upper Nazareth.

Thus the insider becomes the outsider. Not only have the
interpositions between us and Palestine grown more formidable
over time, but, to make matters worse, most of us pass our lives
separated from each other. Yet we live in comradely communication
despite the barriers. Today the Palestinian genius expresses itself in
crossings-over, in clearing hurdles, activities that do not lessen the
alienation, discontinuity, and dispossession, but that dramatize and
clarify them instead. We have remained; in the words of Tawfik
Zayyad's famous poem, 'The Twenty Impossibles,' it would be
easier 'to catch fried fish in the Milky Way,/to plow the sea,/to teach
the alligator speech' than to make us leave. To the Israelis, whose
incomparable military and political power dominates us, we are at
the periphery, the image that will not go away. Every assertion of

*Tyre, South Lebanon,
1983. Rashidyé camp: A
local official collects
messages from the
relations of refugees for
the International Red
Cross.*

41

our nonexistence, every attempt to spirit us away, every new effort to prove that we were never really there, simply raises the question of why so much denial of, and such energy expended on, what was not there? Could it be that even as alien outsiders we dog their military might with our obdurate moral claim, our insistence (like that of Bartelby the Scrivener) that 'we would prefer not to,' not to leave, not to abandon Palestine forever?

Kalandia (near Ramallah), 1967. A few days after the end of the June War: in the foreground, an Israeli officer, lost in thought. Behind the window, a young villager.

Jerusalem, 1979. A dialogue between left-wing Israeli and Arab intellectuals.

The proof of whatever small success we have had is not that we have regained a homeland, or acquired a new one; rather, it is that some Israelis have admitted the possibility of sharing a common space with us, in Palestine. The proposed modes of such a sharing are adventurous and utopian in the present context of hostility between Arabs and Jews, but on an intellectual level they are actual, and to some of us – on both sides – they make sense. Most Palestinians have their own special instance of the Israeli who reached out across the barricade most humanly. For some it is the intrepid Israeli lawyer defending Palestinian political prisoners, or trying to prevent land expropriations and collective punishment; for others it is – the testimony of Salah Ta'amari, leader of the Palestinian prisoners rounded up during the Israeli invasion and put in the Ansar prison camp, comes to mind – an Israeli in a position of authority (prison guard or army officer) who prevented some atrocity or showed some clear sign of humanity and fellow feeling. For my part, removed from the terrible pressures of the scene, I think of all the Israeli (or non-Israeli) Jews whose articulate witness to the injustice of their people against mine has marked out a communal territory. The result has usually been a friendship whose depth is directly proportional to the admiration I feel for their tenacity of conscience and belief in the face of the most slanderous attacks. Surely few have equaled the courage and principle of Israel Shahak, of Leah Tsemal and Felicia Langer, of Noam Chomsky, of Izzy Stone, of Elmer Berger, of Matti Peled, of so many others who stood up bravely during the events in Lebanon.

43

Nazareth, 1979.
A municipal kindergarten,
looked after by nuns.

There are few opportunities for us Palestinians, or us Palestinians *and* Israelis, to learn anything about the world we live in that is *not* touched by, indeed soaked in, the hostilities of our struggle. And if it isn't the Palestinian-Zionist struggle, there are the pressures of religion, of every conceivable ideology, of family, peers, and compatriots, each of them bearing down upon us, pushing, kneading, prodding every one of us from childhood to maturity.

In such an environment, learning itself is a chancy, hybrid activity, laced with the unresolvable antitheses of our age. The child is full of the curious hope and undirected energy that attract the curatorial powers of both church and state. Fortunately, here the spirit of the creative urge in all human activity asserts itself – neither church nor state can ultimately exhaust, or control, the possibilities latent in the classroom, playground, or family. An orderly row of chairs and tables, a disciplined recitation circle in a Catholic school with a nun in charge, are also places for the absorption of more knowledge and experience than authorities impart – places where the child explores here and there, his/her mind and body wandering in space and time despite the constraints in each. In a school where the teacher is a devout Muslim, the child's propensity for disturbing or opposing the schemes of knowledge and discipline causes him/her to leave the table, disrupt the pattern, seek unthought-of possibilities. The tension between teachers and students remains, but better the tension than the peace of passivity, or the unresisting assent to authority.

Amman, 1984. Camp at
Baqa'a, one of the oldest
in Jordan. The YWCA
looks after some of the
kindergartens.

44

STATES The pressures of the here and now require an answer to the Palestinian crisis here and now. Whereas our interlocutors, our 'others' – the Arab states, the United States, the USSR, Israel, our friends and enemies – have the luxury of a state in which institutions do their work undisturbed by the question of existence-or-not, we lead our lives under a sword of Damocles, whose dry rhetorical form is the query 'When are you Palestinians going to accept a solution?' – the implication being that if we don't, we'll disappear. This, then, is our midnight hour.

It is difficult to know how much the often stated, tediously reiterated worries about us, which include endless lectures on the need for a clear Palestinian statement of the desire for peace (as if we controlled the decisive factors!), are malicious provocation and how much genuine, if sympathetic, ignorance. I don't think any of us reacts as impatiently to such things as we did, say, five years ago. True, our collective situation is more precarious now than it was, but I detect a general turning inward among Palestinians, as if many of us feel the need to consolidate and collect the shards of Palestinian life still present and available to us. This is not quietism at all, nor is it resignation. Rather, it springs from the natural impulse to stand back when the headlong rush of events gets to be too much, perhaps, for us to savor life as life, to reflect at some distance from politics on where we came from and where we are, to regrasp, revise, recomprehend the tumultuous experiences at whose center, quite without our consent, we have been made to stand.

Jerusalem, 1984.

Near Senjel, a village between Ramallah and Nablus, 1979.

Jean Mohr's photograph of a small but clearly formed human group surrounded by a dense and layered reality expresses very well what we experience during that detachment from an ideologically saturated world. This image of four people seen at a distance near Ramallah, in the middle of and yet separated from thick foliage, stairs, several tiers of terraces and houses, a lone electricity pole off to the right, is for me a private, crystallized, almost Proustian evocation of Palestine. Memory: During the summer of 1942 – I was six – we rented a house in Ramallah. My father, I recall, was ill with high blood pressure and recovering from a nervous breakdown. I remember him as withdrawn and constantly smoking. My mother took me to a variety show at the local Friends school. During the second half I left the hall to go to the

47

toilet, but for reasons I could not (and still do not) grasp, the boy-scout usher would not let me back in. I recall with ever-renewed poignancy the sudden sense of distance I experienced from what was familiar and pleasant – my mother, friends, the show; all at once the rift introduced into the cozy life I led taught me the meaning of separation, of solitude, and of anguished boredom. There was nothing to do but wait, although my mother did appear a little later to find out what had happened to me. We left immediately, but not before I furtively took a quick look back through the door window at the lighted stage. The telescoped vision of small figures assembled in a detached space has remained with me for over forty years, and it reappears in the adjusted and transformed center of Jean's 1983 picture. I never ventured anywhere near that part of Ramallah again. I would no more know it than I would the precise place of this photo; and yet I am sure it would be familiar, the way this one immediately seemed.

My private past is inscribed on the surface of this peaceful but somehow brooding pastoral scene in the contemporary West Bank. I am not the only one surveying the scene. There is the child on the left who looks on. There are also the Swiss photographer, compassionate, curious, silent, and of course the ever-present Israeli security services, who hold the West Bank and its population in the vise of occupation. As for those terraces and multiple levels: Do they serve the activities of daily life or are they the haunted stairs of a prison which, like Piranesi's, lead nowhere, confining their human captives? The dense mass of leaves, right and left, lend their bulk to the frame, but they too impinge on the slender life they surround, like memory or a history too complex to be sorted out, bigger than its subject, richer than any consciousness one might have of it.

The power grid recalls the Mercedes in Tripoli. Unassimilated, its modernity and power have been felt with considerable strength in our lives here and there throughout the Third World. Another childhood memory: Driving through the Sinai from Egypt into Palestine, we would see the row of telephone and electricity pylons partnering the empty macadamized road that cut through an even emptier desert. Who are they, I would ask myself. What do they think when we are not here? When we stopped to stretch our legs, I would go up to a pole and look at its dull brown surface for some sign of life, identity, or awareness. Once I marked one with my initials EWS, hoping to find it again on the trip back. All of them looked exactly the same as we hurtled by. We never stopped. I never drove there again, nor can I now. Futile efforts to register my presence on the scene.

Intimate memory and contemporary social reality seem
connected by the little passage between the child, absorbed in his

private, silent sphere, and the three older people, who are the public world of adults, work, and community. It is a vacant, somewhat tenuously maintained space, however; sandy, pebbly, and weedy. All the force in the photograph moves dramatically from trees left to trees right, from the visible enclave of domesticity (stairs, houses, terrace) to the unseen larger world of power and authority beyond. I wonder whether the four people are in fact connected, or whether as a group they simply happen to be in the way of unseen forces totally indifferent to the dwelling and living space these people inhabit. This is also, then, a photograph of latent, of impending desolation, and once again I am depressed by the transience of Palestinian life, its vulnerability and all too easy dislocation. But another movement, another feeling, asserts itself in response, set in motion by the two strikingly marked openings in the buildings, openings that suggest rich, cool interiors which outsiders cannot penetrate. Let us enter.

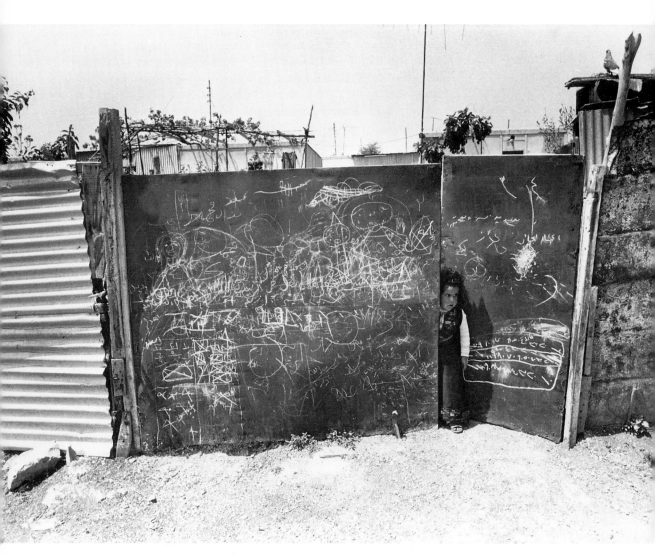

Doorway, Jarash camp, near Irbid, 1983.

2 Interiors

The phrase *min al-dakhil,* 'from the interior,' has a special resonance
to the Palestinian ear. It refers, first of all, to regions of the interior of
Israel, to territories and people still Palestinian despite the
interdictions of the Israeli presence. Until 1967, therefore, it meant
the Palestinians who lived within Israel; after 1967 the phrase
expanded to include the inhabitants of the West Bank, Gaza, and
the Golan Heights, and since 1982 it has also meant the Palestinians
(and Lebanese) of South Lebanon. The most striking thing about
this meaning of *al-dakhil* is the change in value that has taken place
in its connotation. As recently as the early 1970s, I can recall, Israeli
Palestinians were considered a special breed – someone you might
easily be suspicious of if you were a member of the exile or refugee
Palestinian population residing outside Israel. We always felt that
Israel's stamp on these people (their passports, their knowledge of
Hebrew, their comparative lack of self-consciousness about living
with Israeli Jews, their references to Israel as a real country, rather
than 'the Zionist entity') had changed them. They weren't like us in
the sense that as Arabs living in the Arab world, subject to the heady
triumphs and weepy sorrows of Arab nationalism, we were leading
a life independent of imperialism and Zionism. They were different
in a pejorative sense.

Now they are still different, but privileged. The people of the
interior are cherished as Palestinians 'already there,' so to speak,
Palestinians whose lives on the edge, under the gun, inside the
barriers and *kasbahs,* entitle them to a kind of grace denied the rest of
us. It is also true, alas, that since 1970 our collective history *fil-kharij*
('in the exterior') or in the *manfa* and *ghurba* ('exile' and
'estrangement') has been singularly unsuccessful, progressively
graceless, unblessed, more and more eccentric, de-centered,
alienated. We Palestinians lost our status in Jordan, Lebanon, Syria,
and Egypt. Of course, the PLO is recognized by over one hundred
countries, and we have a whole sheaf of U.N. resolutions to our

credit, but no one has any illusions about our real status as outcasts, and failures to boot. A look at our balance sheet reveals massacres, expulsions, and demotions on one side of the ledger, and practically nothing on the other, the credit side. And, to jump to another metaphor, not only is the writing on the wall ominous, but we're not sure what it is trying to tell us.

Therefore, those in Palestine, in the interior, who experience Israeli rule directly, are in a sense better off than those of us who can only *talk* about Zionism while experiencing the unlovely solicitude of our Arab brethren on the outside. Politically, it is important to note that Palestinian activity is now mainly directed toward and focused on the interior, whereas until the 1982 Israeli invasion of Lebanon, the problems and politics of the exterior were what mattered most.

The second meaning of *al-dakhil* is slightly more complicated. It refers to privacy, to that region on the inside that is protected by both the wall of solidarity formed by members of the group, and the hostile enclosure created around us by the more powerful. Two Palestinians meet for the first time, let us say in Delhi or London, and strike up a conversation. Within a minute or two, and with no explicit questions or answers, they can determine each other's original residence, their type of work, their political persuasion (even the deviation or current within that), and their value system – all of them conveyed in a set of specific words or phrases, names, inflections, and emphases, known *only* to Palestinians. But to be on the inside is also not to be yourself on the outside: You have to participate in and speak the language of the outside world, which means that you have to use 'their' codes, but to mean something quite different. But the problem of the inside is that it *is* inside, private, and can never be made plain or evident to anyone, perhaps not even to one's fellow members. The world of secrecy, of private existence, of cabals and conspiracies is a fact of most societies. In Arab tradition it is almost always colored by religion, both Muslim and Christian, but in ways that, I think, are much more subtle and nuanced than most Orientalists (or outsiders) have suspected. Even when it appears that insiders or initiates know the codes, they are never sure whether these codes can in fact deliver the right answers to the important questions, can confirm the stability of what is or gain the assent of the whole group. Thus, although to Palestinians today the word *awdah* ('return') is crucial and stands at the very heart of our political quest for self-determination, to some it means return to a Palestinian state alongside Israel, yet to others it means a return to *all* of Palestine.

To be on the inside, in this sense, is to speak from, be in, a situation which, paradoxically, you do not control and cannot really be sure of even when you have evolved special languages –

*Doorway, village of
Shafa'amr, Galilee, 1979.*

sometimes evasive, always idiosyncratic – that only you and others
like you can understand. The structure of your situation is such that
being inside is a privilege that is an affliction, like feeling hemmed in
by the house you own. Yes, an open door is necessary for passing
between inside and outside, but it is also an avenue used by others
to enter. Even though we are inside our world, there is no
preventing others from getting in, overhearing us, decoding our
private messages, violating our privacy. That is how we read the
history of Palestine, from the Crusades to Balfour and Weizmann:
that it was entered despite us, and lived in despite us.

What do you do then? You try to get used to living alongside
outsiders and endlessly attempting to define what is yours on the
inside. We are a people of messages and signals, of allusions and
indirect expression. We seek each other out, but because our interior
is always to some extent occupied and interrupted by others –
Israelis and Arabs – we have developed a technique of speaking
through the given, expressing things obliquely and, to my mind, so
mysteriously as to puzzle even ourselves.

53

Sidon, 1983. Ein el-Hilwé camp. The boys show off their strength, skill, and combativeness.

Example: The cult of physical strength, of fascination with body-building, karate, and boxing, which has been a striking fact of life among Palestinian youth for quite a while, is obviously the response of the weak to a strong, visibly dominating other. But it is also an eye-catching, almost decorative pattern woven through ordinary experience, and it means something much more than 'making ourselves strong.' It is an assertion of self, an insistence on details beyond any rational purpose. But what may appear to outsiders as utter stupidity for us scores a tiny, almost imperceptible point on the inside, as it were.

The following story illustrates my meaning. The wife of a distinguished European literary figure wrote me some time ago of their visit to Jerusalem; he was lecturing at the university, as was she, I think. They were there for six weeks. During that time she said they'd only met Palestinians twice, of which one meeting was the occasion for her letter. The man 'in charge of a shop [selling

54

embroidery] in David Street' engaged her in conversation, in between bargaining over some merchandise. It appeared that he was 'an acquaintance and admirer' of mine: It was clear to me that he had volunteered this information in response to her telling him in a perfectly natural but quite irrelevant way that she knew Edward Said. She had undertaken then 'to send on . . . the enclosed message,' which was written in Arabic on a small bit of paper torn out of a spiral notebook. My friend also noted the man's wish to register Palestinian superiority over the Arabs in all things (intelligence, martial arts, trading), a superiority expressed by him in the phrase 'we are the Jews of the Arab world.' In all this my correspondent accurately sensed 'rhetorical nuances and complications which I [she] was too unsituated to understand,' especially since she was accompanied by an Israeli friend for whose benefit much of the man's performance was carried on.

In a camp north of Ramallah, 1979. A youth club where, as in prison, it is vital to keep in good physical shape.

55

After all this, what was the message to me? I confess to a certain excitement as I unfolded the tiny bit of paper, and also to a self-congratulatory feeling about the esteem in which I was held by people who didn't know me but who nevertheless valued the contribution I was making to our cause. To begin with, the message was headed by my name in roman script. There followed five lines of Arabic, telling of the writer's great expertise in karate and of his participation in the world karate championships 'under the name of Palestine.' There was nothing else. But, I thought, how typical of Palestinian insiders' communications – that odd bravado, not really meant to be a joke. The exchange of messages came almost naturally to both of us, given our situations. He was inside, and using the good offices of a sympathetic outsider to contact me, an insider who was now outside Jerusalem, the place of our common origin. That he wrote my name in English was as much a sign that he too could deal with the world I lived in as it was that he followed what I did, with some pride, perhaps, but also with the wariness of one who for too long has been 'represented' by Westernized intellectuals whose track record wasn't any too good. The time had come to demonstrate a healthy indication that the Edward Saids had better remember that we were being watched (by karate experts), somewhat approvingly, but also cautiously. Finally, his (to me) comic insistence on his physical skills revealed the same, often uninspired, assertion of self all of us seem to possess. He had already done his super-Palestinian routine for my friend, and probably knew that she would tell me; now he was doing it again, knowing that I would repeat the story. I have.

Such networks of witnesses, testimonials, and authorities threaded through our dispersed community amplify our assertions with such insistence as to be positively numbing. To outsiders this assertiveness is frustrating, not only because of its obduracy, but also because it seems to renew itself ceaselessly, without ever producing anything new or anything outside it that might be illuminating. To me, and to others like me who live in the *manfa* ('exile') or *ghurba* ('estrangement'), there is nevertheless something reassuring (if a bit inane) about those on the inside – in Palestine or in the Arab world, which is closer than New York or Berlin to *al-dakhil* – repeating familiar patterns to the point where repetition itself becomes more important than what is being repeated. In the rigorous discipline of the repetition, as my karate expert knew perfectly, you cannot get out of it, cannot easily transform it into a symbol of something else. Karate does not stand for self-development, but only for the repeated act of being a Palestinian karate expert. A Palestinian. It is as if the activity of repeating prevents us, and others, from skipping us or overlooking us entirely.

Jerusalem, 1979. Bus station.

This compulsion to repeat is evident in the interiors of Palestinian houses of all classes. The same food and eating rituals organized around a table or central space occur with maddening regularity. The rituals of offering and hospitality are designed, I think, to be excessive, to put before a guest more than is needed, more than will be consumed, more than can be afforded. Wherever there are Palestinians, the same signs of hospitality and offering keep appearing, the same expectant intimacy, the same displays of affection and of objects – replicas of the Mosque of Omar, plates inlaid with mother-of-pearl, tiny Palestinian flags – appropriated for protection as well as sociability. Naturally, they authenticate and certify the fact that you are in a Palestinian home. But it is more than that. It is part of a larger pattern of repetition in which even I, supposedly liberated and secular, participate. We keep re-creating the interior – tables are set, living rooms furnished, knick-knacks arranged, photographs set forth – but it inadvertently highlights and preserves the rift or break fundamental to our lives. You see this if you look carefully at what is before you. Something is always slightly off, something always doesn't work. Pictures in Palestinian houses are always hung too high, and in what seem to be random places. Something is always missing by virtue of the excess. I do not

Jenin, 1984.

Tripoli, Badawi camp, 1983.

58

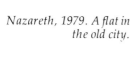

Nazareth, 1979. A flat in the old city.

mean that the result is tragic or sad; to the contrary, the rift is usually expressed as a comic dislocation, the effect of too much for too little a space or for too uninteresting an occasion. Too many places at a table; too many pictures; too many objects; too much food. My own rather trivial version of this tendency toward disproportion and repetition is that I always carry too many objects – most of them unused – when I travel, which I do frequently. Every time it occurs, the repetition introduces an almost imperceptible variation. Each of us, I believe, recognizes the pattern in her- or himself, and in others.

60

Amman, 1984. Memories of Jerusalem: Pictures, picture books, looking at pictures.

This pattern of similarly unbalanced, but always infinitesimally varied, interiors will ultimately attract the attention of the outside observer – as it has caught Jean Mohr's eye – but I doubt that deeper reasons for it are easily explained. Yes, the oddness of these excesses, and asymmetries, their constitutively anti-aesthetic effect, their communicated insecurity seem to symbolize exile – exile from a place, from a past, from the actuality of a home. But, there is yet another problem being expressed in this form of repetition.

Palestine is a small place. It is also incredibly crowded with the traces and claims of peoples. Its legacy is one not just of conquest and resettlement, but also of reexcavations and reinterpretations of history. Glenn Bowersock, the classical historian, describes this history aptly as the 'deliberate fragmentation of a fundamentally unified region.' The novelty of Bowersock's approach is that because of his special focus on pre-Zionist and pre-Islamic early Palestine, he is able to perceive beyond all the jostling and shoving 'the fact of an Arabian state and subsequently an even more extensive Palestinian state in the Middle East' during the period from Alexander's death to the coming of Islam.

The original spaciousness of that region disappeared, alas, with the arrival of a whole army of nineteenth- and twentieth-century foreign claimants to Palestine. Instead, topographically and even bibliographically, the place is unimaginably divided, dense, and cluttered. Cover a map of Palestine with the legends, insignia, icons, and routes of all the peoples who have lived there, and you will have no space left for terrain. And the more recent the people, the more exclusive their claim, and the more vigorous the pushing out and suppressing of all others. In addition, each claim invents its own tradition, its own dynastic filiations, causing still more deflections, shoving matches, and dislocations: The already overcrowded map now seethes with violently conflicting forces, raging over the surface.

We, too, have lost the sense of space. We think of Palestine not as 'an extensive Palestinian state' but as a small, extremely congested piece of land from which we have been pushed. Every effort we make to retain our Palestinian identity is also an effort to get back on the map, to help those *fil-dakhil* to keep their precarious foothold. This is a secular effort – as are most of the struggles of our own recent political history – and I would insist that religious considerations are secondary, are consequences, not causes. But the map, like the land itself, or like the walls of our houses, is already so saturated and cluttered that we have had to get used to working within an already dense and worked-over space. Far from being innovators, we are late-comers, a people in the late twentieth century trying to gain the right of self-determination that everyone else has (even the Falklanders, juridically at least, have what we still seek). We do what everyone does, therefore; there is no novelty about us. Our efforts seem like adornments to what is already adorned.

Ramallah, 1984.Portrait on a crowded wall.

Hebron, 1979.
The tomb of Abraham,
serving as both a mosque and
a synagogue, with a military
guard.

Every direct route to the interior, and consequently the interior itself, is either blocked or preempted. The most we can hope for is to find margins – normally neglected surfaces and relatively isolated, irregularly placed spots – on which to put ourselves. We can only do so through much perseverance and repetition (so many have already done this ahead of us) and in the knowledge that our distinction may well appear at the end and after much effort as a small nick, a barely perceptible variation, a small jolt. Irony. Imposition. Odd decorum.

Tel-Sheva, 1979.

As our situation has worsened, our closely managed acts of self-assertion have grown odder, more ironic, and darker. During the Israeli invasion of Lebanon, the conquerors would periodically put a captured Palestinian – male, able-bodied, potentially a troublemaker – on the radio, and make him go through paces for the benefit of other Palestinians. This was a propaganda exercise to which, on the West Bank and in South Lebanon (the areas whose inhabitants were the targets of the exercise), Palestinians had no comparable response or propaganda apparatus of their own. Insofar as they could respond, they had to do so through the already ongoing discourse of the Israeli interrogation itself, as in the dialogue that follows here, translated from the colloquial Arabic. Note the deliberately stupid miming tactics of the hapless, but by no means witless, prisoner:

INTERIORS   Israeli broadcaster: Your name?
Captured Palestinian *fedayi* ('guerrilla'): My name is
Ahmed Abdel Hamid Abu Site.
I.B.: What's your movement name?
Pal.: My movement name is Abu Leil ['father of night'].
I.B.: Tell me, Mr. Abu Leil, to which terrorist
organization do you belong?
Pal.: I belong to the Popular Front for the Liberation
[*tahrir*] – I mean Terrorization [*takhrib*] – of Palestine.
I.B.: And when did you get involved in the terrorists'
organization?
Pal.: When I first became aware of terrorism.
I.B.: And what was your mission in South Lebanon?
Pal.: My mission was terrorism . . . in other words, we
would enter villages and just terrorize. And
wherever there were women and children, we
would terrorize. Everything and all we did was
terrorism.
I.B.: And did you practice terrorism out of belief in a
cause or simply for money?
Pal.: No, by God, just for money. What kind of cause is
this anyway? Why? Is there still a cause? We sold out
a long time ago.
I.B.: Tell me, where do the terrorist organizations get
their money?
Pal.: From anyone who has spare money for terrorism; in
other words, from the Arab regimes that support
terrorism.
I.B.: What's your opinion of the terrorist Arafat?
Pal.: I swear that he's the greatest terrorist of all. He's the
one who sold us and the cause out. His whole life is
terrorism.
I.B.: What's your opinion of the way the Israel Defense
Forces have conducted themselves?
Pal.: On my honor, we thank the Israel Defense Forces
for their good treatment to each terrorist.
I.B.: Do you have any advice for other terrorists who are
still terrorizing and attacking the IDF?
Pal.: My advice to them is to surrender their arms to the
IDF and what they'll find there is the best possible
treatment.
I.B.: Lastly, Mr. Terrorist: Would you like to send a
message to your family?
Pal.: I'd like to assure my family and friends that I'm in
good health, and I'd also like to thank the enemy
broadcasting facility for letting me speak out like
this.
I.B.: You mean the *Kol Israel,* the Voice of Israel?
Pal.: Yes sir, thank you sir, naturally sir.

65

If you want a terrorist, given that all Palestinians who opposed Israel in Lebanon are terrorists, then any Palestinian you get is a terrorist, a 'terrorist' with a vengeance. The ideological mufflers of the interrogator's mind are so powerful as to shut out any alertness to the Palestinian's parody of terrorism: Each line he speaks repeats and, by rhetorical overkill, overdoes what his interrogator wants from him. Buried in the black comedy of his performance is his message, which cannot speak straight out but must lie in wait to be perceived by others. This story and several others like it circulate among Palestinians like epics; there are even cassettes of it available for an evening's entertainment.

Damascus, 1983. Two boys at the camp at Sayida Zeinab.

I am reminded also of the late poet Mu'in Basisu's autobiographical *Descent into the Water*, which describes life in the Gaza Strip during the fifties, when it was ruled by Egypt. Basisu was a young militant in the Palestinian Communist Party who passed his formative years in a series of Egyptian jails. These travails took place entirely within an Arab (and not an Israeli) setting, which makes the irony of Arab 'nationalists' abusing those very Palestinians whose cause is at the center of their nationalist concerns, all the more pronounced. Still more ironic for Basisu is the fact that his guards are Palestinians. When he and his companions come to the Cairo prison, 'the secret police guards expressed joy at seeing us. Perhaps for one second in five years the Palestinian secret policeman pauses to remember that he is a Palestinian, but then he resumes writing his reports against Palestinians.'

Palestinians are cast in the roles set for them by other Arabs. Basisu's jailers are 'mimic men,' although for one infrequent second their roles allow a break from the dreadful routine into which they have been fitted and to which they have become accustomed.

The dynastic sense, the feeling for one's immediate past, the effort of placing ourselves in a living continuum: there is little help to be gotten for such things. The closeness and clutter of the present force us to attend to the details of everyday life. Whenever I look at what goes on in the interior I am always surprised at how things seem to be managed normally, as if I had been expecting signs of how different 'they,' the people of the interior, are, and then find that they still do familiar things. We Palestinians conduct ourselves, I think, with an energetic consciousness that there are still chores to be done, children to be raised, houses to be lived in, despite our anomalous circumstances.

Druze family in Galilee, 1979.

67

I am obsessed with how as a people we got here. In early 1982 I
spent several weeks with a British film crew, recording life in a
South Lebanon refugee camp for Palestinians. The sequences were
to be part of a television documentary called 'The Shadow of the
West,' which concerned the essentially imperialist relationship of
Britain, France, and the United States to the Arabs. A central
component of the film was a look at a spinoff of that relationship, the
question of Palestine. Many of the Palestinians I spoke to and filmed
in South Lebanon were younger than I; Lebanon was all they really
knew, so they deferred to the older people on matters historical. On
two occasions I became perturbed by the inadequacy of our history
and the way we use it. Once an old man was prodded into
reminiscences of life in Palestine by a group of his young male
relatives. He spoke about it very elaborately – the village he grew up
in, the family gatherings, feasts and memorable occasions, the
pleasures of being at home. But when I asked how it ended, how he
became a refugee, he suddenly stopped. Then he got up and left.

    The second occasion concerned an old woman who, along with a
group of her nieces and daughters, was cheerily regaling me with
advice about what, as a Palestinian living in America, I should be
doing. Make a revolution, one of them said; have more children,
said another, implying that the two I had so far produced testified at
best to an impaired manhood and patriotism. Then we got on to life
in Qasmiyeh, the refugee camp we were in. None of the women felt
they would be there for long, as, after all, they didn't belong there.
Then I turned to the old woman, Um Ahmed, and said: 'How did
you get here?' She paused for a moment, as if such a question was a
surprise, and then rather offhandedly said, 'I don't really know; I
just found myself here.'

    But for the people who live in or near the interior where it is
impossible to deny their Palestinian origins, there is at least the
privilege of obduracy. Here we are, unmoved by your power,
proceeding with our lives and with future generations. These
statements of presence are fundamentally silent, but they occur
with unmistakable force. When you compare them with the
cautious worried glance of Palestinians in the West you cherish
them more. Recently I was driving back to New York along Route 1
in New Jersey and stopped at a filling station. The attendant's
accented English spoke to me, as it did probably to no one else that
day, of a Palestinian, a middle-aged, frighteningly busy man who
never looked up from his pumps or his clipboard. 'You're an Arab,' I
said in Arabic. 'Yes, yes,' he replied with a sudden elevation of his
bent head. 'Where from, what place, what town?' I pursued him.
'Jordan,' he quickly returned. 'But you're Palestinian, aren't you?'
'From Nablus,' he said, and then he moved away from me, busy
still. It hurt me, his apparent unwillingness to declare himself, and I

Ramallah, 1984. Proudly displayed, the picture of a man first sentenced to life imprisonment, then expelled to Algeria and then to Jordan.

wanted to resume our conversation with a few words about not being ashamed to admit our backgrounds. . . . But perhaps he suspected me of being some sort of spy. In any event, he was too far away and too preoccupied with getting things done to give me more notice.

When my thirteen-year-old, Wadie, and I were in Amman, he would ask everyone he met whether he or she was Jordanian or Palestinian. One bearded taxi driver with a strong Palestinian accent answered, 'Jordanian,' to which Wadie impatiently shot back, 'Where in Jordan exactly?' Predictably the answer was Tul-Karm – a West Bank town – followed by a verbose disquisition on how 'today' – the occasion being that famous 1984 meeting of the Palestinian National Council held in Amman, at which King Hussein spoke –

there was no difference between Jordanians and Palestinians. Wadie, perhaps sensing my sullen disapproval of the driver's waffling and reacting to my unusual reluctance to press the point, insisted otherwise. 'There *is* a difference,' he said, only at his age he couldn't quite articulate it. For our pains the man drove us at least five miles out of our way, and then dumped us at the edge of the city. 'Get someone else to take you back!'

It isn't wrong, I think, to comprehend these lapses about the past as the result of two forces. One is the bewildering and disorienting present. Look at the maze of uncertainties, conflicting predicaments, untidy overlappings of Palestinian life in Palestine. Look at it with some sense of what it means to negotiate it. You will immediately see its symbolic analogue in any panoramic overview of contested sites such as Gaza or even Amman, where the patchwork of overbuilt and structureless dwellings offers little perspective or direction. Everything seems packed in without regard to symmetry, form, or pattern. The second is that the past for all of us Arabs is so discredited as to be lost, or damned, or thought about exclusively in contrast to the present and a not too credible projection of the future. Perhaps this just amounts to the same thing, except that we tend too readily to grant the future (which is at best ambiguous) an aura of legitimacy. After all, as the Lebanese literary critic and novelist Elias Khoury has said, the legitimacy of the future is built almost solely on the illegitimacy of the past – that seemingly limitless series of failures, invasions, conspiracies, destructions, and betrayals. And after you've listed them all, there is not much more to say, so you say nothing. This in turn has allowed the entire apparatus of the modern Arab state, tyrannical and lusterless in equal parts, to propose itself as the legitimate guarantor of the future and, more important, the legitimate ruler of the present. Israel has tried to do the same thing, but for Palestinians the Jewish state has no moral legitimacy. Because they keep promising a bright future, Arab states do have some, but it is dwindling very fast.

〰〰〰〰〰

But once another power – Arab, European, or Israeli – invades your interior, dismisses your past, and stakes its claims on your future, perhaps it does not make any difference who or what that power is. I am not a great believer in the claims of ethnos, tribe, blood, or even patria, but I must, I feel, make the distinction between the varieties of invasion. It is a matter of what, say, the Israeli does not allow us that the Arab, highly ambivalent about us, does. Maybe it is simply a matter of degrees of alienation, or of various dialects of the same language (Arabic) versus totally different languages.

Gaza, 1979, refugee camp: The tents have slowly been replaced by brick buildings with corrugated-iron roofs.

Settlement of Ramot, near Jerusalem, 1979. As the buildings neared completion, tenants were in short supply.

The attitude expressed in the construction of settlements on the West Bank is unmistakable. Visually there is a rude interventionary power in them that, I am told, shocks even Israelis. One thinks not only of a coarse army of heedless and rough crusaders, but also – given some of the structures themselves – of a marching cancer. As for the effect on the landscape and Palestine's ecology, the offense is deep and lasting.

Palestine's Arab identity – and I am perfectly willing to grant that it has other identities too – was and is being rewritten and defaced, as when you scrawl across a perfectly legible page and turn it into something ugly and offensive. This process continues with results, at a great distance from Palestine, that hurt a great deal. One example: *New York* magazine reports cleverly in its 'Intelligencer' column (by one Sharon Churcher) on a national costume show of forty nations put on by UNESCO at its Paris headquarters. Included was a display of Palestinian embroidered dresses, the kind that have always been made and worn by Palestinian women. The title of Churcher's piece, however, was 'Terrorist Couture,' presumably because as a member of UNESCO, the PLO was responsible for supplying the exhibit of Palestinian dresses.

Churcher implies that the PLO was hijacking Palestinian culture, and that UNESCO fell for it. She quotes Owen Harries (the Australian who led the successful Heritage Foundation campaign to get the United States to leave UNESCO), who accuses UNESCO of using the national costume ploy 'to convince the U.S. they [the PLO] are changing' – presumably from a Communist front to a legitimate cultural agency. Churcher then draws upon her large fund of knowledge for the *coup de grâce*: 'UNESCO may not have that good a fix on terrorist couture: It showed the "Sunday best" of an upper-middle-class Bethlehem lady, a Middle East expert observed.'

If you sort out the plague-on-all-your-houses aspect of this item, you'll see a number of things suggested. First of all, we are led to believe that the Palestinians never had folk, popular, or authentic native costumes; the dresses exhibited are only the Sunday dress-ups of the upper middle class. Second, the PLO and UNESCO, both scoundrels, are in league, the former lying about its people, the latter either complicit or ignorant, or both. Finally, the small picture of one of these costumes is not allowed to speak for itself. It is described as 'upper middle class' by an unnamed 'expert,' and just

The foreground drops away, leaving only the Arab village, its mosque and houses surrounded by fruit trees, olive trees, and stone walls.

74

in case the point of the PLO-UNESCO deceit is missed, the whole discussion is herded under the rubric of 'terrorist couture.'

The facts are that the picture is indeed of a Palestinian woman's dress, that it is a kind made and used by all classes, and that there exists an extensive anthropological and folkloric literature on such dresses, almost any item of which would have confirmed the PLO's fulfillment of UNESCO's charge that costumes should be national, popular, genuine. In a small way, one can see the mischievous dirt-doing of the item (which is part of a much more complex and extensive pattern). Everything about Arab Palestine is rewritten. Turn it into something extremely suspect, show that it is connected to terrorism, or ridicule it and push it away derisively. There are no Arab Palestinians. The land did not exist as Palestine, and perhaps the people did not exist either. 'We Palestinians' have almost imperceptibly become 'they,' a very doubtful lot.

A story like that always evokes a kind of tired bitterness in me. Who, in the great scheme of things, is Sharon Churcher? She produces a few lines of column in a frivolous magazine, and I feel impelled to bring logic, history, and rhetoric to my aid, at tedious length. We need to retell our story from scratch every time, or so we feel. What we are left with when we get to scratch is not very much, and memory alone will not serve. This seems to be the point from which Jabra Jabra's powerful novel, *The Search for Walid Massood* – an extraordinary work of late-blooming Palestinian sensibility – takes off: that memory is not enough. The 'innocence and ambiguity' of memory, Jabra writes, require sentences that correspond to that memory exactly. But no such sentences exist, and they would take years to produce, with very doubtful results. 'What has been cogently thought,' Adorno says, 'must be thought in some other place and by other people. This confidence accompanies even the loneliest and most impotent thought.' That is another way of phrasing the Palestinian dream: the desire for a perfect congruence between memory, actuality, and language. Anything is better than what we have now – but still the road forward is blocked, the instruments of the present are insufficient, we can't get to the past.

Still, I am impressed by some of the methods used to restore Palestine in the meantime. There is the steady trickle of memoirs: the daybooks, journals, albums, diaries, and recollections of various Palestinians. All of them rely on the notion of statement – enunciations grounded in personal authority – and strive for the clarity of unquestioned evidence. The journals of Akram Zuayter; Hisham Sharabi's somber autobiography, *Al Jamr wa'l Rumad* (*Ashes and Embers*); the testimony of Zakaria al-Shaikh on resisting the Sabra and Shatila massacres in his eyewitness report, as a camp-dwelling refugee, of the 1982 inferno. Others I have read and been

impressed with arise from, as it were, a scene of regular life inside

*Acre, 1979. Open-air café
at the port.*

Palestine (*min dakhil Filastin*) – the harrowing, episodic narrations of
Raja'i Buseilah, a blind Palestinian poet and scholar, who recounts
his experiences as a child in 1948 forced to leave Lydda (thanks to the
prodding of the then Hagannah commander, Yitzhak Rabin); Walid
Khalidi's immense compilation of largely personal photographs of
Palestinians during the period between 1876 and 1948, *Before Their
Diaspora*; Shafik al-Hout's memories of Jaffa, 'The Bride of
Palestine'; the little encyclopedia produced a couple of years before
he died by Shafik's father-in-law, Ajjaj Nouweihid, *Rijal min Filastin*
(*The Men of Palestine*), a work of affectionate compilation that recalls
Abbasid biographical dictionaries and in which I found reference to
my father's family.

76

And yet, I recognize in all this a fundamental problem – the crucial absence of women. With few exceptions, women seem to have played little more than the role of hyphen, connective, transition, mere incident. Unless we are able to perceive at the interior of our life the statements women make – concrete, watchful, compassionate, immensely poignant, strangely invulnerable – we will never fully understand our experience of dispossession.

I can see the women everywhere in Palestinian life, and I see how they exist between the syrupy sentimentalism of roles we ascribe to them (mothers, virgins, martyrs) and the annoyance, even dislike, that their unassimilated strength provokes in our warily politicized, automatic manhood.

Damascus, 1983. The camp at Sayida Zeinab: refugees from wars of 1948, 1967, 1973.

When my mother speaks of her early life in Nazareth – her immensely strict father's special gentleness with her, her closeness to her mother and her subsequent alienation from her, the (to me) rural authenticity of their life there, an authenticity with which I have had no contact – I have always sensed in her an apprehension of the regretted and unbridgeable gap separating her from that life. Not that she was driven from Nazareth in 1948 – she wasn't. She left with my father in 1932. But she tells this story. Immediately after she and my father were married at the mandatory government's registry office, a British official ripped up her passport. 'You will now travel on your husband's passport,' he said. To her remonstrations and queries he replied, in effect, 'this negation of your separate identity will enable us to provide a legal place for one more Jewish immigrant from Europe.'

Too symbolic, and too definitive perhaps a tale of woman's disenfranchisement in a colonial situation. I do not know how frequent such practices were, and whether there was some absolute correspondence between the disappearance of my mother's distinct legal identity and the appearance of a Jewish settler. The experience itself of the ripped-up passport is too searingly painful and graphic not to have remained vivid for over fifty years in my mother's life, and she tells the story with great reluctance, and even shame. As her son I have sympathetically preserved the episode, a tender hurt endured in consequence of her new identity as my father's wife, my mother and the closest companion of my early years. I have therefore interpreted her trauma as the sign that she passed from full immediacy of being – the fullness of being that comes from her person as a young Palestinian woman – to a mediated and perhaps subsidiary person, the wife and the mother.

Later I realized that being such a mediated person, distributed among a number of important but secondary roles, is the fate of all Palestinian and Arab women; this is the way I encounter them, and the way they exist in our various societies. Certainly these are general social and historical facts, but their particular meaning in Palestinian life, given our special situation, is unusually intense. The question becomes how to see the woman's predicament: Is she subordinated and victimized principally because she is a woman in Arab, Muslim society, or because she is Palestinian? However the question is answered, there is an urgent need to take stock with equal precision of the woman's negation and the Palestinian's dispossession, both of which help to constitute our present situation.

The sense of my mother's story as a just representation of the Palestinian woman's plight struck me with great intensity when I saw a documentary film by the young Palestinian director Michel Khleifi. Like my mother, Khleifi was born and grew up in Nazareth. Now a resident of Brussels carrying an Israeli passport, he, too, is an exile. In a number of ways his film, *The Fertile Memory*, responded to the need I feel for restitution and recognition when I think of my mother's experience and all it implies.

Khleifi puts before us two Palestinian women who live as subjects of Israel. One of them, his aunt, Farah Hatoum, is an elderly widow who remained in Nazareth after 1948. We see her working in an Israeli bathing-suit factory, riding a bus, singing a lullaby to her grandson, cooking and washing. The sequences of her at work show a combination of very close detail and highly concentrated repetition, especially in household chores of the sort normally taken for granted by other family members. The impression one gets of this almost frighteningly concrete expenditure of energy is that it sustains life in ways that are just below the threshold of consciousness. One feels a peculiar respect for its protracted discipline, a respect that the effusively male character of Palestinian nationalism doesn't ordinarily permit. The woman's loneliness, the menial offices to which she is consigned, the essentially tending nature of her work, the fineness of her tasks (sewing among them), all suggest a truer condition of Palestinian life than our articulate discourse normally discloses.

Hebron, 1979. A grocer's shop in the market of the old city.

*At home in a refugee
shantytown, outside the
village of Ramah, Galilee,
1979.*

The centerpiece of the film is a dramatization of the old woman's relationship to the land. This is done in the two connected scenes that build her into a potent symbol for what has been called 'internal exile,' a condition already in evidence during the period of the British mandate, when my mother was stripped of her passport. Farah is first shown in conversation with her adult children, both of whom are trying to convince her to sell land that she owns but that in fact has been 'repossessed' by Israelis. Although she still holds the title deed, she well knows it is only a piece of paper. Now her children tell her that legal advice has convinced them that despite the expropriation by the Israelis, there is an opportunity to sell the land to its present tenants: Apparently someone wants to legalize her dispossession by giving her money in return for final entitlement.

She'll have none of it. A large, jowly woman, she sits rocklike at the kitchen table, unmoved by the logic of financial well-being and peace of mind being offered her. No, no, no, she says. I want to keep the land. But you don't actually have it, is the rejoinder which makes those of us living in exile quietly feel even more sympathy for her, since she at least continues to assert the value of some, any, connection with the land. But just as quickly, the woman's stubbornness reminds us that our mementos, memories, title deeds, legal claims simply accentuate the remove at which we now live. In the various cocoons provided by exile there may be room symbolically to restore discrete parts of our heritage; and yet, the discrepancies between symbol and reality remain, as when the finest collection of Palestinian dresses is preserved, catalogued, and reproduced by Wadad Kawar in Amman, published in Japan, ignored and overlooked by American columnists who instead trade in the easy coin of 'terrorist couture.' Of course, the land is not truly ours.

Refugee camp, Sidon,
1983.

Farah resumes her statement thoughtfully and feelingly, 'I don't have the land now, but who knows what will happen? We were here first, then the Jews came, and others will come after them. I own the land. I will die. But it will stay there, despite all the comings and goings.' This is a logic that defies understanding on one level; on another, it is deeply satisfying to her. Thus we also remember the many instances of a repeated stubbornness that makes no sense, such as proclaiming 'here I stand' surrounded by the icons of our glorious failures (Abdel Nasser chief among them) – or that makes only enough sense to distinguish our side of the line from theirs.

Later in *The Fertile Memory* Farah is taken to see her land for the first time in her life. This is perhaps a curious thing but, as Khleifi once explained to me, not so unusual for a woman of that generation whose late husband had owned the property, cared for it, and willed it to her when he died. When she came into it she had already been dispossessed, and for all that her title deed has done for her, she might have been in Syria displaying pictures of the Hanging Gardens of Babylon.

Somehow, Khleifi has managed in his film to record Farah's first visit to her land. We see her step tentatively onto a field; then she turns around slowly with arms outstretched. A look of puzzled serenity comes over her face. There is little hint on it of pride in ownership. The film unobtrusively registers the fact that she is there on her land, which is also there; as for the circumstances intervening between these two facts, we remember the useless title deed and Israeli possession, neither of which is actually visible. Immediately then we realize that what we see on the screen, or in any picture representing the solidity of Palestinians in the interior, is only that, a utopian image making possible a connection between Palestinian individuals and Palestinian land. Farah's reconnection with her land, merely formal though it is, called up, and even calmed, the painful memory of my mother and the identity taken from her in 1932. An aesthetic experience a generation later, partially healing the wound.

The other major figure in *The Fertile Memory* is Sahar Khalifé, a successful young novelist and teacher from Nablus. Her presence is by no means nostalgic or inarticulate. Of a younger generation than Farah, she is more self-aware, both as a woman and as a Palestinian. She describes herself as a militant, though with considerable irony. But even Sahar's life is more impressive than Farah's – she too is dispossessed, her identity undercut: as a nationalist, by the structure of Israeli power holding the West Bank; as a divorced working woman, by the conventions of the predominantly Muslim and traditional community of Nablus. She expresses alienation from political and, to a degree, sexual fulfillment; both have been denied her, the first because she is a Palestinian, the second because she is an Arab woman. Nevertheless, Sahar is securely in place. One feels about her, and other Nabulsis, that – Israeli occupation, and political and social tensions notwithstanding – they are securely in place, their lives are led where such lives have always been led.

It is Khleifi's achievement to have embodied certain aspects of Palestinian women's lives in film. He is careful to let the strengths of Farah and Sahar emerge slowly, even if at a pace that risks losing the film the larger audience it deserves. He deliberately disappoints the expectations engendered in us by the commercial film (plot, suspense, drama), in favor of a representational idiom more innovative and – because of its congruence with its anomalous and eccentric material – more authentic. Each of us bears fragmented memories of the experiences of the generation whose culminating tragedy was dispossession in 1948. To these experiences Farah Hatoum is allowed to speak. Each of us senses the subtle undercutting that takes place on the shadow line between two worlds. To this, Sahar Khalifé gives expression.

But Khleifi does not give in to the editorial manipulation that, for example, Farah's real situation – and his, as her compatriot – might have provoked. Her daily existence is not portrayed as taking place directly against the standard scenes of Israeli domination. There is barely a glimpse of Israeli soldiers, none of Palestinians being rounded up by police. He even resists the temptation to italicize the significance of Sahar's more militant, if still subdued, position. No cuts to scenes of Palestinian activism, tire-burning, or rock-throwing.

Instead, Khleifi has given the women's lives an aesthetic clarity which, for me, a male Palestinian, sheds new light on our experience of dispossession. Yet because I am separated from those experiences by time, by gender, by distance – they are, after all, experiences of an interior I cannot inhabit – I am reconfirmed in my outsider's role. This in turn leads me, defensively perhaps, to protect the integrity of exile by noting the compromises of life in the Palestinian interior – the forgetfulness and carelessness that have historically characterized the losing battle with Zionism, the too close perspective that allows thoughts to be unthought, sights unrecorded, persons unmemorialized, and time thrown away.

·····················

Here is another face of a woman spun out with the familiarity of years, concealing a lifetime of episodes, splendidly recorded by a listening photographer. It is a face, I thought when I first saw it, of our life at home. Six months later I was showing the pictures casually to my sister. 'There's Mrs. Farraj,' she said. Indeed, it was. I first saw her in 1946 when my cousin married her daughter, who was the first beautiful woman I encountered in real life. Then I saw her in the fifties, and then again now, in Jean Mohr's picture. Connected to me, my sister, my friends, her relatives, her acquaintances, and the places she's been, her picture seems like a map pulling us all together, even down to her hair net, her ribbed sweater, the unattractive glasses, the balanced smile and strong hand. But all the connections only came to light, so to speak, some time after I had seen the photograph, after we had decided to use it, after I had placed it in sequence. As soon as I recognized Mrs. Farraj, the suggested intimacy of the photograph's surface gave way to an explicitness with few secrets. She is a real person – Palestinian – with a real history at the interior of ours. But I do not know whether the photograph can, or does, say things as they really are. Something has been lost. But the representation is all we have.

·····················

84

Amman, 1984. Mrs. Farraj.

3 Emergence

A significant segment of Arab Palestinian history has been made up of peasant farming and agricultural life. Through the nineteenth century rural settlement accounted for at least 65 percent of Palestine. At the center of life, of course, stood the village, although among the small number of Arab nomads within Palestine it was the clan that mattered most. Pastoral and rural forms of existence dominate in our society. The chances are today that one out of every two Palestinians you meet is descended from farmers or shepherds, and has deep roots in a land worked by small rural communities.

It is therefore very tempting to think of this life as essentially timeless and anonymously collective. I am perhaps an extreme case of an urban Palestinian whose relationship to the land is basically metaphorical; I view the Palestinian rural community at a very great remove. I know that my father's family is Jerusalemite but that a century and a quarter ago it derived from a Nazareth Christian clan, which may have been close to the land; my mother originally comes from a Safad family – the Bishoutys – of uncertain occupational background before the mid-nineteenth century but, I believe, artisans and professionals rather than landworkers. In any case my knowledge of my immediate relatives, friends, and acquaintances is so crowded with doctors, business people, and professionals (teachers, professors, lawyers, writers, clerics) as to eclipse any direct relationship with the majority rural population of Palestine. If I also factor in my long residence in the United States, as student and now academic, with increasingly infrequent visits to the Middle East, whatever tenuous childhood relationship I may have had with Palestinian village or farm life is pretty much dissipated. So even though I can still note the largely agricultural roots of our society, these have no direct personal immediacy for me. I continue to perceive a population of poor, suffering, occasionally colorful peasants, unchanging and collective.

But this perception of mine is mythic, and further (de)formed by the specific inflections of our history and the special circumstances out of which my identity emerged. For example, I, like many Palestinians, am the product of a society of names constructed and trafficked in according to European norms. Yet this is a new society: It was not the one my father was born into and grew up in. My name is Edward W. Said, the W. being for my father's name, Wadie, changed to William when he was naturalized as an American citizen. His name, as I knew it, was Wadie Ibrahim Said; when, however, I was a student at St. George's School – a mission school in Jerusalem, which belonged to the Anglican episcopate and in whose parish I was baptized – I could see that my father's name as a member of the school's soccer and cricket teams in 1910 was inscribed on the honor tablets as simply Wadie Ibrahim. Later I realized that names in traditional use were restricted to parental

Overleaf:
The last nomads: at the edge of the desert, near Bersheeba, 1979.

88

Farmwork, between Haifa and Ramah, 1979.

Amman, 1983. Baqa'a camp.

functions, as in Abu Wadie ('father of Wadie') and Im Abdullah ('mother of Abdullah'); or to the identification of parents, as in Wadie Ibrahim, Ibrahim being my grandfather's name; or to clans, tribes (Khleifawi, Ta'amari), or villages (Ramlawi, Nabulsi). Names restricted us to these circles, made our identities either so local as to be intelligible only to a very small group, or so general as to indicate only one's region or province. Like the *Said* my father adopted when he returned to Palestine in 1920 after several years in the United States, the given names that exist today are the product of the British mandate (1922), the Zionist presence, the national awakening – forces requiring countable statistics and reified (and hence taxable) populations, divisions, and classifications.

The sudden resurgence during the late sixties and seventies of names like Abu Ammar, Abu Jihad, Abu Firas, etc, was a reversion to the old ways, a search for a more essential Palestinian identity. Directly linked to the rise of the armed resistance movement, these noms de guerre symbolized the act of taking possession of ourselves in *our* way, rather than in ways that responded too amenably to the pressures of outside power. Only now, of course, the relative anonymity of a name like Abu Ammar ('father of Ammar') coexisted alongside the distinctiveness of one as well known as Yasir Arafat. The recuperation of our past by its partial re-creation in the present was obviously a political act: The plethora of Abus meant first that those who adopted the name were affiliated to political organizations, and second, that they were Palestinian traditionalists. Affiliation and filiation were, so to speak, in coalescence.

The effect of this revivalism on the peasant with a *kaffiyah,* who had always been and was still called Abu Mohammad or Abu Jaafar, was a mixed blessing. His choices were either to remain an obscure figure, known only to his immediate relatives, friends, and fellow villagers, or to become a potential recruit to one or another political organization.

Any awareness of the past, of historical change, of one's own way of seeing, must affect the way one reads the pictures of peasants. Now the faces you see looking out on the world exude not so much the resignation of passively endured oppression as the reserve of something withheld from an immediate deciphering. This man lives in the enormous Amman refugee camp of Baqa'a. The things you can be sure of have to do with what he can do – he's a worker, a peasant – and where he comes from (his village, his family, his past and present movements). But he does not simply express the poignant, mute, and enduring sadness of an archetypal peasant people, without politics, or historical detail or development. In such a face we can now discern something different: the reserve of a force building up out of a long, intense history, frustrated and angry about the present, desperately worried about the future.

Look again at the shepherds, the women in the fields, the man with a *kaffiyah*; add to these Mohr's earlier photograph from 1950 of a single file of peasant women in Irbid. They are all, in a troubling sense, without the marks of an identifiable historical period. And for that matter, they could be scenes of people anywhere in the Arab world. Placeless. Yet all the photographs are of working people, peasants with a hard life led on a resistant soil, in a harsh climate, requiring ceaseless effort. We – you – know that these are photographs of Palestinians because I have identified them as such; I know they are Palestinian peasants, and not Lebanese or Syrian, because Jean has been my witness. But in themselves these photographs are silent; they seem saturated with a kind of inert being that outweighs anything they express; consequently they invite the embroidery of explanatory words.

Peasant women in Irbid, 1950.

What's more, in our heads legends arise unbidden which further obscure the photographs. The unadorned fact that they show working people of the peasant class is constantly compromised by bits of prose floating across their surfaces. 'Shepherds in the field,' says one such tag, and you could add, 'tending their flocks, much as the Bible says they did.' Or, the two photographs of women evoke

Near Mount Carmel, 1979. Village women return from collecting wood.

phrases like 'the timeless East,' and 'the miserable lot of women in Islam.' Or, finally, you could remember something about the importance to 'such people' of UNRWA, or the PLO – the one an agency for supplementing the impoverished life of anonymous Palestinians with the political gift of refugee status, the other a political organization giving identity and direction to 'the Palestinian people.' But these accumulated interpretations add up to a frighteningly direct correlative of what the photographs depict: alienated labor, as Marx called it, work done by people who have little control of either the product of their labor or their own laboring capacity. After such a recognition, whatever bit of exotic romance that might attach to these photographs is promptly blown away. As the process of preserving the scenes, photographic representation is thus the culmination of a sequence of capturings. Palestinian peasants working are the creatures of half a dozen other processes, none of which leaves these productive human beings with their labor intact.

The most famous of early-twentieth-century European books about Palestine is Philip J. Baldensperger's *The Immoveable East*. Voluble, packed with information – ethnographic detail, folk wisdom, peasant lore – it is magisterial in its indifference to the problems of interpretation and observation. The son of an Alsatian missionary, Baldensperger was a beekeper as well as a folklorist. Baldensperger does pack in more information about the Palestinian peasantry than can be found anywhere else, and with the work on the village of Artas by Hilma Granquist, a Finnish archaeologist and anthropologist, we have as good an archive of material on the workings of the Palestinian countryside as we are likely to get.

Yet, reading Baldensperger and Granquist, seeing their photographs and drawings, I feel at an even greater remove from the people they describe.

Jerusalem, 1979. A permanent market in the Old City.

> As a rule, the Fellahin are dark brown, black-haired and have long, broad beards, differing in this respect from the Bedawin, whose beards are scanty and adorn the chin only. Certainly, in a country so often invaded by outsiders, there is a tinge of foreign blood. Here and there, and especially near big centres, you may be surprised to meet fair or even red-haired individuals. But the principal type is the brown one, with a thick, hooked nose, a round head, thick lips and bones, broad shoulders, large hands and, as a rule, well in muscle – neither too fat, nor too thin. The women are slightly smaller, with elegant bodies, strong hips, good-sized breasts, almost small feet and hands, dark eyes and long, thick black hair. Fellahin and Fellahat usually wear a plain long shirt with wide sleeves which reaches, when not held up by a girdle, to the feet.

What I think of as I read passages like this in Baldensperger is the almost total absence of Palestinian writing on the same subject. Only such writing would have registered not just the presence of a significant peasant culture, but a coherent account of how that culture has been shaken, uprooted in the transition to a more urban-based economy. I am told that one Tawfik Canaan, used by Europeans as a native informant, was an impressive ethnographer of his own people, but so far as I have been able to determine none of his work is easily available. Why this absence? Did we never care about ourselves? How do we register the passing of time, the product of our work, the changes in our history? While *they* were traveling, observing, writing studies and novels, paying attention to themselves, what were we doing? It is as if after decades of backbreaking work, much pain, and the miseries of poverty, disease, and ignorance, we were able only to transport ourselves from the field to the marketplace, a dingy, miscellaneous, and untidy repository of produce strewn about in hopes that it will catch

94

Acre, 1979. Near the old harbor, an engine is being repaired. Nothing is ever too old to be saved.

Onion farmer, near Jenin, 1984.

someone's eye – a passing businessman's, a dawdling boy's, a timid housewife's – there to be consumed on the spot, and thence to disappear. Beginning again yields precisely the same short little passage.

The contrast between their urge to record and systematize and our passive, scattered incoherence comes up again and again in our history. Compared to the brilliantly comprehensive Zionist system of organization for Jewish settlement in Palestine, for example, our national efforts to maintain ourselves economically in Palestine relied essentially upon the individual – a stalwart farmer here, a good doctor there. You can see the whole tragic, almost completely aborted history of our working people in its individual embodiments: the onion grower, the car mechanic, the construction worker, the domestic servant, the schoolteacher, the petty government or commercial clerk, the shepherd, the businessman, the intellectual, the peddler or small shopkeeper. Very occasionally these people were supported by something more than their own efforts, most notably by the PLO which, since 1970, has existed as a national apparatus for directing and protecting working Palestinians from the lonely ravages of market, war, and exile. Much of the time, however, they have had to go it alone, relying upon the uncontrolled forces of politics and opinion to bring them returns for their labor. The standard reference book on the Palestinian economy before World War II, Said Himadeh's *Economic Organization of Palestine,* registers the stark difference in organization, pay, and power between Jewish and Arab workers; the former had the Histadrut – the federation of labor unions – and a wealth of services sustained and directed by European-minded, committed Zionists, whereas our people were either in the fairly unenlightened clutches of a quasi-feudal landowning class or, in the case of urban workers, left to fend for themselves because unorganized. The result is that Arab wage rates are essentially determined by supply and demand, and vary with the locality.

The situation in 1938 was idyllic compared to what has occurred since. Most Palestinian workers under Israeli jurisdiction today are concentrated in the very lowest segment of the wage-earning classes; they are construction workers, mechanics, furniture-makers, woodworkers, upholsterers, all located within what has been called the secondary, or labor-intensive, labor market, the primary market being mainly in strategic or military industries and open only to Jewish workers. Salaries for Arabs in Israel are based on the Histadrut scale; salaries for Palestinians from the Occupied Territories are considerably lower than for Jews. But it is the contrast in working conditions – everywhere – that is most dramatic.

Approximately 70 percent of the Arab work force travels to work in Jewish locales, according to sociologist Elia Zureik, and the figure is close to 90 percent among workers between the ages of fifteen and twenty-five. In many instances the cost of travel wipes out most of the wages, since we are not permitted to stay overnight in predominantly Jewish areas; indeed, within the green line (pre-1967 Israel), some Israeli employers lock in Arab workers from the Territories between the hours of 2:00 and 6:00 A.M.

As a result we are a migratory and impoverished labor force in our own country. There is a flourishing market in Arab child labor from the poorest areas like Gaza, and the economic depression in Israel has turned the Arab daily wage laborer into a disconsolate, transportable commodity, loitering in the marketplace until picked by a Jewish labor entrepreneur for piecework elsewhere.

Nazareth, 1979. Five o'clock in the morning, the city's main street. Arabs seeking work wait to be signed up for the day — perhaps at a farm or factory on the other side of the country.

Nazareth, 1979. Waiting.

*Nazareth, 1979. A
discussion of wages, then
departure for work.*

Yet the Palestinian works anyway, often without much hope or horizon, with the result that alienation from work is now gradually being assimilated and transformed into a prevailing attitude, described and characterized by Raja Shihadeh, a gifted young West Bank lawyer and writer, as *sumud*, 'to stay put, to cling to our houses and land by all means available.' Work first becomes a form of elementary resistance, a way of turning presence into small-scale obduracy. You accept the narrowness of opportunity as a given, and you consider change, for the foreseeable future, as bringing worse, rather than better, conditions. Work then becomes a daily articulation of the formidably precise status quo into which you are bound; it brings you to a performance of your actual condition that, you find, sparks your consciousness of what you are all about, where you are to be found, how maddeningly complicated are the mechanisms that surround you. Raja Shihadeh says that sometimes at that very point you discover your freedom, which is neither capitulation nor 'blind, consuming hate,' but a sense that 'your mind is the one thing that you can prevent your oppressor from having the power to touch.'

Cares and anxiety set in nevertheless. The moment of unguarded reflection is also the moment of deepest vulnerability. Will the children be picked up for taunting the settlers? Will 'they' take another piece of land? Limitless worries, for which there is no truly effective antidote except going about your work tomorrow, again, beginning again.

El Bireh, 1984. Craft center.

Acre 1979. Carpenter-cabinetmaker.

Observe two striking differences between Zionism and the Palestinian national movement. In getting things done (mainly acquiring territory), Zionism was actually a Benthamite policy of detail, whereas the Palestinian tendency – scarcely a 'policy' – was to make a stand on unassailable general principles, which never prevented the ground from being literally cut out from underneath us. The result of this is that Zionists have a state, Palestinians don't. Of course it is true that Zionism proved the militarily stronger of the two antagonists, and that it also had broad principles upon which to rely, but the focus of mobilization was definable in relatively small terms – 'another goat and another acre,' as Chaim Weizmann said.

I remember being stirred as a boy by accounts of how, when the time came and the British mandate ended, the Zionists would be driven away by our valiant Hebronites (the proverbial Palestinian strongmen), who needed only sticks to shoo them all back to where they came from. But what I also remember were the endless discussions, testimonial declarations, and protestations about the justice of our cause, and the visual evidence, which is still very clear in my memory, of row upon row of Jewish farmers, schoolchildren, pedestrians even, going about their business with their backs turned, so to speak, to the urgent, aimless life among the Arab Palestinians whose much larger land holdings proved later to be meaningless. No detail, no itemization in Arab existence as in Jewish life, no organization of the sort that made a percentage of one's cinema ticket price go to the Jewish Agency. What we had – and still have – were our markets and native places: untidy, undocumented, unexpressive.

Jerusalem, 1984. Old City, Arab sector.

A second difference follows interestingly from the first. Because the Diaspora by definition was not in Palestine, a great deal of what was done in the Promised Land on Zionism's behalf was also presented – perhaps *projected* is the better word here – as if onto a kind of world theater stage. The acre and the goat, the hospital and the school, the settlements themselves: All these seemed to be not just happening, but taking place as part of a drama the world was

102

witnessing, a drama about the reconstruction – or, as Weizmann called it, the 'reconstitution' – of Palestine. For the Diaspora this drama had very different meanings at different times. It was always meant to be a didactic alternative picture to the traditional view of Jews in the West. Later the redemptive message of the reconstruction was changed to meet the situation created after the concrete horrors of the Holocaust: Palestine as refuge, as affirmative action for those dispossessed Jews not massacred by Nazi Germany.

Nablus, 1979. The market.

Still later there came the view of Zionists as early founding fathers and pioneers, then as Spartans, then as existential heroes. Some of this self-conscious drama was caught recently by the Israeli novelist Amos Oz, who said: 'For as long as I live, I shall be thrilled by all those who came to the Promised Land to turn it either into a pastoral paradise or egalitarian Tolstoyan communes, or into a well-educated, middle-class Central European enclave, a replica of Austria and Bavaria.' Not only was Zionism to restore Israel, then, it was also to show the world that Jews could be Bavarians,

103

Tolstoyans, or Marxists in Asia, in the midst of land that, as the literature has it, had been 'neglected' for centuries. One is reminded of the near surrealism of the white-suited accountant in Conrad's *Heart of Darkness* who, oblivious to the 'great demoralization of the land' in darkest Africa, continues his Londoner's routine, 'devoted to his books which were in apple-pie order.'

But there *were* other people already in Palestine, and the slow accumulation of land by a policy of detail as well as the painstaking drama of the state taking shape before the world's eyes came more or less to blot out the natives. Until 1948, less than 7 percent of Palestine was Jewish-owned; only eight out of Palestine's sixteen subdistricts contained more than 1 or 2 percent Jewish land ownership, and in those eight the numbers were never more than 35 and 39 percent (in Jaffa and Haifa, respectively) and usually less than 20 percent. Yet about 77 percent of Palestine became Israel – that is, land under the sovereign authority of a state declared to be 'the state of the Jewish people,' without officially declared boundaries – David Ben-Gurion having purposely (according to his biographer Michael Bar-Zohar) left out of his announcement of the state's birth in May 1948 any reference to its actual international borders. Not all the land within Israel was rid of Arabs or Arab ownership right away. Most of it was in time, by a process of carefully drafted, ruthlessly applied Absentee Property Regulations; 40 percent was immediately confiscated by a stroke of the pen. By 1950 a culminating summary land law was passed: the Absentee Property Law, which entitled the Israeli custodian of 'absentee property' to sell Arab lands more or less at will. The irony was of course that the Palestinians were not, in any permanent sense, 'absent': The large numbers (about 780,000) driven out into neighboring states would have willingly returned had they been allowed to do so. Approximately 160,000 remained as non-Jewish Israeli citizens. On the one hand refugees, on the other, 'present absentees,' to use the official Israeli designation. The process continues: In the Occupied Territories over 50 percent of the land has now been expropriated. Development is forbidden, permits for building are extremely scarce, and water and electricity are controlled by Israel, with the result that well over 15,000 Palestinians a year are forced to emigrate. The massive daily influx of unskilled Palestinian workers into Israel, estimated at 90,000, further impoverishes life in the Territories. The remaining local industry in the West Bank tends to be small, family-owned, without much of a market, and dependent upon remittances from abroad by Palestinians working elsewhere (in the Arab world, Europe, the United States).

The smile in adversity continues, nevertheless.

Tyre, South Lebanon, 1983. Refugee in Rashidyé camp.

Why these natives in all their untidy backwardness could not impress the Zionists, much less the rest of the world, with their presence is something I still cannot really understand. Certainly one important answer is the blindness of the Zionists. There are clear parallels between Zionists and American Puritans, say, or between Zionists and nineteenth-century European theorists of 'empty' territory in Asia and Africa. But what is still more perplexing is how the same blindness is repeated painstakingly by modern Zionist historians who retell the story, not with the wisdom of hindsight, but with the exact same narrowness of vision that spurred on the early Zionists. The latest version of this view of us by some American Zionists – Joan Peters and supporters of hers like Saul Bellow and Barbara Tuchman – is that we *never* existed, and that so-called Palestinians are illegal immigrants from neighboring Arab states who came to Palestine between 1946 and 1948, drawn there by the prosperity of Jewish colonies.

But there are other causes which implicate us more directly. Surely Zionism's genuine successes on behalf of Jews are reflected inversely in the absence of a major history of Arab Palestine and its people. It is as if the Zionist web of detail and its drama, in alliance with our own inability and recalcitrance to dramatize and speak about ourselves, screened the Palestinians not only from the world but from ourselves as well. And indeed, as political scientist Ibrahim Abu-Lughod has written, Palestinians for a decade after 1948 adopted a politics of accommodation to the Arab and Israeli realities all around them; they became Egyptian Palestinians, Lebanese Palestinians, or Israeli Palestinians of the sort whose life Sabri Jiryis has chronicled in *The Arabs in Israel* (1976), a book that exemplified the process – it was originally written in Hebrew using Hebrew sources by a Christian Palestinian law graduate of the Hebrew University. During the Nasser period, Palestinians were caught up in a general wave of Arab nationalist sentiment, what Abu-Lughod calls 'a politics of rejection.' The negative enthusiasm of those years echoed the *no*'s of the Khartoum Summit of 1967: no recognition of, no negotiations with, no surrender to Israel. Then after 1967, Palestinian nationalism asserted itself as a separate phenomenon in the breach made by the Arabs' defeat. In a new movement that has been called the politics of revolution and hope, the massive campaign of self-help began: Palestinians threw off their tutelage, armed themselves, and announced their program of self-determination and self-renewal.

But in all these phases, with the exception of a handful of literary works (among them the poetry of Mahmoud Darwish, Samih al-Qassem, and Tawfik Zayyad, a small number of stories and one novella by Ghassan Kanafani, Emile Habibi's satiric novel, Fawaz Turki's autobiographical memoir, and Mu'in Basisu's Gaza diary),

106

the concrete human detail of Palestinian existence was sacrificed to big general ideas. I have long believed, for instance, that our insistence on 'armed struggle' – originally a phrase symbolizing the Palestinian will to fight unremittingly and on our own for our political rights – very quickly turned into a worship of fetishized military postures, guns, and slogans borrowed from theories of the people's war in Algeria and Vietnam. This ritualized and gross emphasis on arms caused us to neglect the incredibly complex and far more important political and cultural aspects of our struggle, and it played right into the hands of Israel, which with its superior propaganda apparatus turned everything we did against its occupation of our lands, its devastation of our villages, and its oppression of our population, into 'terrorism.'

Still, these pessimistic and critical things by no means tell the whole story of what is in fact a remarkable rise out of destitution. The general Palestinian opposition to Israeli exclusionary practices has become a potent symbol of what it means to be an adversary to the seedy status quo everywhere in the Middle East. Palestinians were hailed as models and heroes by Iranians in 1978 and 1979, as they had been previously by Egyptian students and intellectuals,

Jerusalem, 1984. An anxious conference about land.

107

Syrian workers, and Third World liberation groups. The emergence of the P L O – always hovering between revolutionary ideals and the more practical aims of a national independence movement – brought forth in many different places an array of Palestinian institutions (schools, factories, hospitals, research and publication networks) that have responded sensitively to the scattered quality of Palestinian life today. The central fact remains of course: We are a people without a land of our own. But for the first time in our history, one can see Palestinians as Palestinians in a sense *producing themselves* as they go about their work in a new environment of Palestinian self-consciousness affecting everyone. This self-production has had a noticeable effect. For the first time in its history, Zionism's policy of detail and its dramatic self-protection are faltering, and appear totally inadequate to account for the Palestinian presence.

Nablus, 1979. Soap factory, a traditional local industry.

Take the following examples. Whereas in the early years the Zionists simply ignored the Palestinians, since 1967 they have become strident and openly vicious in tone and substance. Moshe Dayan put it this way in 1978: If Palestinians inside Israel are going to support the P L O, then we shall evict them as we evicted the

108

Nablus soap factory.

*Nablus soap factory. End
of the day.*

Palestinians in 1948. General Eytan (then Israeli Chief of Staff), in an interview with the newspaper *Yedioth Aharonot* (January 19, 1979), had this to say about the Israeli enterprise: 'Before the state of Israel existed we came here [to conquer] this country, and it was for this purpose that the state was established.' Asked about Palestinians in the Galilee, he replied: 'In my opinion, the Arabs today are engaged in a process of conquest of the land, conquest of work, illegal immigration, terror there.' The Galilee, incidentally, is where the largest concentration of Palestinians lives – and has always lived. Such statements are, of course, the background for Meir Kahane's bloodcurdling calls to drive Arabs from all Israel and the Occupied Territories. A cartoon in *Maariv*: Out of an oil drum emanates a huge black genie with a leering face resembling Ayatollah Khomeini's and reflecting all the frightening clichés about Arabs, Muslims, and Orientals in his evil features. This overtly (and paradoxically) anti-Semitic creature is identified as 'Islam – the reaction.' Standing off to the side are a decent-looking, worried gent who represents the West and a little boy wearing a yarmulke. The boy says to his older companion: 'When are we moving?'

Despite our subordinate status, our widely scattered exile, our reduced circumstances, our extraordinary military weakness relative to Israel (and the other Arabs), how is it that we appear so overwhelmingly threatening to everyone?

⁙⁙⁙⁙⁙⁙⁙⁙

The leading Palestinian sociologist – indeed the scholar who has in fact formulated a nascent Palestinian sociology – is Elia Zureik, now professor of sociology at Queens University in Ontario, Canada. Like me, he is a Palestinian Episcopalian, although unlike me he did most of his schooling in Israel. Fluent in Hebrew, Arabic, and English, he articulated his model for the political-economic ground of Palestinian productivity in 1980 when, along with Ibrahim and Janet Abu-Lughod and a few others, he was part of a UNESCO team to develop a blueprint for a Palestinian university based on the actual needs and realities of the Palestinian people. The study was accepted, and it began to be implemented (staff hired, land bought, classes planned) in Beirut – ironically, during the chaotic spring of 1982. Nothing remains of the project today except some valuable documentation, vestiges of which have found their way into other projects, none of them in reality capable of getting past the two problems cited by all other studies: the absence of any secure place or national authority for the realization of Palestinian national life.

Zureik's table of stages in Palestinian history provides a schematic account of how our exile and internal colonialism have worsened

from 1948 to the present.

STAGES	PERIOD	SALIENT FEATURES
Dual society (Zionist colonization)	pre-1948	Asymmetrical power relationships mediated by the British presence, exclusivist Zionist institutions; stunting of Arab economic development; Zionist hegemony and eventual Palestinian dispersion.
Internal colonialism (pre-1967 Israel)	1948–1967	Marginalization of Palestinian peasants; land confiscation; political manipulation; economic stagnation; residential and occupational segregation; duality of economic and social relations.
Dependency of West Bank and Gaza on Jordan and Egypt	1948–1967	Economic and political dependency on Jordan and Egypt; co-optation and political suppression.
Accelerated forms of internal colonialism in Israel; colonial dependency of West Bank and Gaza on Israel	1967–present	Further proletarianization of Palestinians in Israel; economic penetration of West Bank and Gaza accompanied by land confiscation and encouragement of Palestinian emigration; political suppression and denial of Palestinian rights.
Total control by Israel	Future trend	Depopulation of Palestinians through expulsion and emigration; ultimate goal is Zionization of historical Palestine, and, if possible, resettlement of Palestinians in Arab countries.

Once again, though, the bleak picture conveyed by the overall facts does not tell the whole story. It is true that our inferior position to Israel has not improved. But the relationship has changed. What was once a shapeless domination of one people by another has become a series of smaller, more varied configurations. Since 1967 the Occupation has created structures among our people that accentuate, disturb, or disrupt the blanket of power over us. Most, if not all, of these new structures are nationalist, and they have emerged with a starker outline than under Jordanian or Egyptian rule: Greater power produces greater resistance. Most have to do either with building – people and groups who have literally constructed Palestinian institutions – or with ideas, ideas about solidarity, about Palestinian and Arab traditions (*turath*), about self-determination and corporate destiny.

My impressions of these new structures are mixed. On the one hand I consider it one of the most depressing aspects of polarizing Palestine into camps of Jews and non-Jews that each side fortifies the intransigent, ritualistic, and therefore potentially empty nationalism in the other. The dialectic of Jew and non-Jew moves up a notch to a narrower site. It is not enough to assert Palestinianism for its own sake just because Zionism and Israeli state practice have demoted us to third-class status. Indeed, such a response has in some cases had the effect of stunting us politically, so that we tend to view enemies and friends rigidly, in absolute terms – or worse, to suspect each other of compromise, capitulation, collaboration . . . A new vocabulary grows up less for understanding than for reducing the world.

I want to believe, however, that, on the whole, these new changes are both understandable and even genuinely salutary. A new leadership is already in evidence, a leadership not completely based on tribal roots or the web of clan affiliations. These have become less important. Confident, educated, and above all open to the realities of Israel, these new men and women radiate a kind of hopeful security that exiles like myself envy. Their *sumud* is real, concrete, solid: They are *in* Palestine, which is not an idea, as it is for us, but a place. They have forced open the tight little world of the master-slave relationship first introduced in 1967, and have created alternative institutions, like Palestinian cultural centers, that link schools, professional associations, women's groups into confluences of life that parallel those commanded by the Israeli authorities.

Moreover, a class of collaborators has not in fact appeared. Israeli attempts to use tribal patriarchs in the sixties and seventies, and so-called Village League enforcement squads in the seventies and eighties, as tools for creating an apparatus of Palestinian quislings, have failed. Instead, these Israeli strategies–backed up by brutal

Geneva, 1980. United Nations Conference on the Palestinians, with Bassam al-Shaka'a, the former mayor of Nablus, at the rostrum.

police methods that have involved thousands of house demolitions, more than 250,000 arrests, torture, and murder – seem to have strengthened the hold of nationalist leaders whose groups have short-circuited the Israeli power grid in the Occupied Territories. But not without some fearsome casualties. A popular leader like Bassam al-Shaka'a, ex-mayor of Nablus, testifies to his people's plight, only to be scarred irredeemably for that testimony.

The work of *sumud,* from childbearing and building to testifying and fighting, continues. Palestinians, with their nationalist program and their legitimized representative, the PLO, have reopened for Israeli Jews the file closed in 1948 when Palestinian society was destroyed.

Buried inside the archive was the notion that a real people existed, on all sides of which a new state now carried on its business. But since 1967 the appearance of, so to speak, emblematic Palestinians has opened the eyes of some Israelis and tightened the denials of many more. In response to all the symbols of Palestinian explicitness, Israel has promoted a rather fictitious group called 'the terrorists,' who mechanically contain within themselves not merely an identity but a whole systematic discipline of nefarious practices. A veritable industry – operating from institutes in Tel Aviv and Washington for the study of terrorism, furnished with experts, seminars, and endless documents – now churns out a 'science' called counterterrorism, the product of an appalling doctrinal reductiveness applied to an already scandalous dehumanization of the Palestinian; this has justified Israeli mass terror against even the idea of Palestinian nationalism, joined in by air force, army, navy,

113

Geneva, 1980. Mr. Shaqa'a, victim of an attack that cost him both legs.

administrative rhetoric, and scholarship, on a scale so large it caricatures our actual strength. The distortion recalls Swift's abrupt juxtaposition of large and small in the first and second voyages of *Gulliver's Travels*. Thus the dismissible terrorist is Lilliputian on the one hand; on the other hand, the efforts at dehumanization and miniaturization are so obsessive they inflate the threat unimaginably. The Palestinian as resident of Brobdingnag.

I do not like to call it a Palestinian *diaspora*: there is only an apparent symmetry between our exile and theirs. Besides, the Diaspora no longer exists spiritually and culturally as it once did in Central Europe, with tragic figures like Kafka, Schoenberg, and Benjamin at its core. Today's Diaspora is represented centrally by American Zionism, a far different phenomenon. The screaming hostility, the glib language of dismissal and contempt, the astounding ignorance and guilt – these characteristics of American supporters of Israel, whose power is truly formidable, are marshaled against us in modes of verbal battle that few Israelis would employ. Consequently I find it much easier to debate with an Israeli than an American Jew. In any event, our *ghurba* or *manfa* is a much different thing because, most simply, our demographic ties to Palestine today are more substantial than Judaism's in the period before 1948. Today, of the estimated 4.5 million Palestinians, 1.83 million (40.7 percent) are still in some part of historical Palestine, and 2.665 million (59.3 percent) are elsewhere. Of those elsewhere, there are 1.08 million in Jordan (24 percent); 400,000 in Lebanon (about 8 percent); 250,000 (5.5 percent) in Syria; almost 800,000 (17.8 percent) elsewhere in the Arab world, principally in Saudi Arabia and Kuwait; and 180,000 (4 percent) in the rest of the world.

The biggest concentration of Palestinians, then, is in the Arab world, unlike Diaspora Zionism, which was largely a European phenomenon. Still, the Palestinians' renown for being productive, dedicated, and extraordinarily resourceful workers has – like the reputation of Jews in the West – become something of a legend, not all of it exaggerated. It is manifestly true, for example, that the Palestinians have the highest percentage of university graduates in the Arab world. Similarly, it is true that in the Gulf, but also in Jordan and, until 1982, in Lebanon, Palestinians stand out as teachers, doctors, engineers, entrepreneurs, intellectuals. Daring, a kind of flashy brilliance, a somewhat unstable and insecure aggressiveness – these are some characteristics of Palestinians in their host societies. Often, I am told, Palestinians get secretly blamed for catastrophes.

The Palestinian exiles' present 'success' – de-centered, esoteric, and elusive as it may be – is truly astonishing when contrasted with how badly off we were right after 1948. Most of what I can recall about the early days of the period are obscure boyhood memories of a protracted exposure to the sufferings of people with whom I had little direct connection. My immediate family was completely insulated by wealth and the security of Cairo, where we were living then. Then in the spring of 1948, right after the Deir Yassin massacre, my father's sister and her family appeared from

Amman, 1984. Dr. Bassam Abu-Ghazaleh. Born in Jaffa, he is now dean of the Faculty of Engineering and Technology at the University of Jordan.

Amman, 1984. Mrs. Wadad Kawar, a great collector and specialist in Palestinian crafts, left Palestine for Amman in 1948.

116

Jerusalem, clearly agitated and disturbed at what they had left behind, uncertain about the future; most of my mother's family for its part had moved from places like Jaffa and Safad to the West Bank; later they would move to Amman. I had little grasp of what was occurring in Palestine beyond what I learned from one Jewish classmate in Cairo, Albert Coronel, who once alluded with bitterness to the five Arab states that were fighting the Jews in Palestine. Five against one, he said. I remember well that I said nothing, not knowing exactly what he meant or was referring to, although at the same time my aunt and cousins – of an older generation – spoke about Deir Yassin in frighteningly concrete terms.

These autobiographical snippets serve me as an index of how little I knew at the time about the *nakba* ('disaster'), and yet how definitely I began to discover among Palestinians the force of recovery that took place through work. Because she was a woman of almost superhuman energy and charity, my aunt Nabiha began immediately to dedicate herself to the refugees streaming into

Amman, 1984.
Mr. Nidal M. Sukhtian,
industrialist, born in Nablus,
has been in Amman since
1967.

Paris, 1984. Mr. David
Alphonse, banker. Born in
Jerusalem, he spent fifteen
years in Kuwait and has
been in Paris since 1974.

Egypt. She was a wealthy woman, and so could rely on her own resources to some extent, but as she narrated her experiences to us every Friday at lunch, she was always upset by the unfeeling apparatus of the Arab state, to say nothing of the Egyptian bureaucracy. Palestinians were not given residence permits, work permits, or travel papers. Most were destitute refugees with nowhere to go and nothing to rely on. Nabiha enlisted every conceivable friend or acquaintance to her cause – informally, of course. Schools were pressed to take children; businesses to take the moderately educated; workshops, restaurants, hotels, factories to take the unskilled. I remember that she even found a small group of men jobs as stevedores in Port Said, although she was apprehensive about separating them on weekdays from their wives and children. Once a week she stayed home in order to receive anyone who wanted to see her: The crowds outside her apartment were regularly very large. Most of the rest of the time she and her driver went from place to place in Cairo, starting at dawn and stopping at sunset. She went to houses, to offices, to government centers, to hospitals,

117

clinics, and schools, fixing, cajoling, arranging, haranguing, distributing. She was a tiny, middle-aged woman, widowed, shapeless from the childbearing she endured since her mid-teens, careworn to a degree I cannot forget, and yet she simply charged on with a firmness and a brusque efficiency that on its own modestly personal level carried all before it.

Occasionally she would let me come along, and I would inevitably lag behind her ferocious pace. Much of her time in the awful, decrepit slums she visited would be spent convincing the women left behind with screaming, underfed children that they did *not* need more medicine. Prescriptions and, preferably, money for patent medicines had the status of a miracle cure for these poor women, and it was not until a few years ago that an acquaintance who survived those early days explained to me that what every one of the destitute and powerless looked for was a drug that might induce forgetfulness, sleep, or indifference. Nabiha, however, knew the score from the start, and she had a limitless capacity for understanding and grappling with every complication imaginable. Most of her efforts paid off when she linked better-off Palestinians

Paris, 1984. Mr. Elie Sanbar, the editor of Palestinian Studies, *left Palestine in 1948 for Beirut, then Paris.*

118

with the less fortunate: My father's business, for example, was packed with Palestinians, a great many of whom later went on to considerable prosperity. They remembered my aunt – the Mother of Palestine, she was called – more than they did her brother, although my father never, so far as I knew, turned her down for anything. They were exceptionally close, those two, a pea cut in half, as my mother would often say, not without some jealousy. They were both simple people, driven by unspoken loyalties and dreadful clichés, like 'honesty is the best policy,' which, however banal, achieved in their case an almost transfigured clarity and incorruptible fineness.

My aunt, like my father, had little faith in officialdom. In the years since I came to New York, I have continued to meet people who worked for organizations like UNRWA or CARE, and who knew and admired my aunt. She bandied about the initials – CMS, ICRC, WHO, UNRWA, CARE – as well as the names of the personnel, though she knew in her inarticulately tough way that they weren't at bottom to be relied on. And this is the point she grasped: that the Palestinian must work within the system as well as against it – since every society is going to oppose Palestinians as if by heavenly edict – and be able in some way to create a parallel, or alternative, system that would respond to Palestinian needs.

The simultaneous requirement to identify and to remain apart had its price, of course, especially among the first generation of exiles, who went to great pains to shed their offending (and afflicting) identity in their attempt to melt into the new society. In the early fifties, I saw a disturbing emblem of this conflict in the person of a man brought to my father's office by my aunt. His name was Mostafa, and he was a former police sergeant from Haifa. He was taken on as a sort of supernumerary security man, responsible for the premises in a general way, although he was also used as a messenger and an all-purpose handyman. I had never met a man so apparently broken down and sorry. He had a powerful, athletic frame, yet it seemed, in the unnatural slowness with which he moved, to belong to someone else. He did his work with a flagrant attention to detail that became more pronounced whenever a higher-up happened by. Then he was all bowing and self-effacement and shuffling and dusting and door-opening. Once or twice I saw him when he didn't see me (the superboss's son). Here was an altogether different person. His apologetic shuffle shifted into the stealthy tiptoe of a detective, while his lean body took on the threatening inflections of a man with the law totally on his side. In Mostafa was a prototype of Emile Habiby's al-mutasha'il, that amphibious Pessoptimist: in Mostafa one could simultaneously see the Palestinian at home, so to speak, coexisting with the refugee who was trying to commit a kind of mind suicide.

His children, like those of so many others, were determined to make it through the national education system, which, in Egypt and elsewhere in the Arab world, yielded – if slowly – to the energies of quietly pushy Palestinians. Ten years after he had started with my father, Mostafa had at least three children at Cairo University, all of them studying 'hard' subjects – medicine, engineering, commerce.

The greatest irony is that through this will to work, we Palestinians have in fact accumulated a society – but not in Palestine. The very process that Weizmann had proclaimed for Zionism in Palestine – another acre, another goat – has more or less worked for us everywhere else, although we never really acquired any land. Whether in architecture, or in medicine, or in education, or engineering, or banking, or the fine arts, or in intellectual work, Palestinians are prominent, although anomalously they are to be found in places like Amman, Paris, Washington, Kuwait, and Riyadh. The most striking feature of this society-in-exile is its powerful bourgeoisie, which in the four decades since 1948 has traversed the historical stages lived through in a century and a half by the European bourgeoisie, from Enlightenment, to early industrialization, to capitalism, to late capitalism. The fault that undermines our society, however, is that its center, its seat, its fixed point, is always elsewhere, always a place that we once regarded as intrinsically ours, but that is no longer ours: Jerusalem, Amman, Beirut. The slight hesitation in otherwise aggressive speech, or the tiny, vulnerable opening in the armor of incredible success, or the way, like Wallace Stevens's jar in Tennessee, even our most distinguished citizens pull into sharp focus the eccentricity in every setting: all these perhaps repeat the fault microcosmically.

The far-flung and de-centered Palestinian exile has, of course, brought prominence to members of the new class, and this, in turn, has had some positive influence on the fortunes of thousands of Palestinian laborers, peasants, and camp-dwellers who have been routinely unable to make themselves heard and seen. Nevertheless, these people, buried in the Persian Gulf, or in Ein el-Hilwé camp near Sidon, or in the suburbs and workers' settlements of Tripoli, Libya, are the bulk of our population. No one has studied the relationships between these two groups, although there have been some efforts to look at Palestinian institutions as an index of a functioning, albeit expatriated, society. But the essence of the Palestinian identity has paradoxically been the experience of dispossession and loss, which everyone has lived through and which no one has fully been able to convey. Those of us who live in the West have been conditioned by education and culture to regard exile as a literary, entirely bourgeois state: We think of the great paradigmatic figures like Ovid, Dante, Hugo, or Joyce; we reflect on the inner exile of various modern German or Italian writers; and in so doing we draw elucidation by analogy out of our own smaller-scale exile. But it is the mass of Palestinians dispersed throughout the Near East who, I think, really set the conditions for life in exile, and these are almost by definition silent, indescribable, utterly poignant. Most of us – those who are able to and might perhaps read this book or look at its photographs – have left the other condition behind, but the evidence for it is still there, very far away from amenities like a library, or a salon, or a bank. Our laboring population survives with difficulty – subject to the dictates of bureaucrats and soldiers, prone to disasters and humiliations, more and more dependent on the whims and internal politics of their host countries.

Their history and actuality cannot ever be recovered, but as a people, they can be represented, and they can be connected to their more fortunate compatriots. Arafat did that. As to how he did it, no figures and few facts are of service. In short, I think, he put the Palestinians as a group in circulation. He made it impossible to see the Middle East in general, and Israel in particular, without also seeing the Palestinian. A genius at mediation, at connecting disparate segments of Palestinian life, he and the PLO have drawn to themselves a staggering amount of attention, disproportionately negative from his enemies for whom he is both archtraitor and

Geneva, 1983. Yasir Arafat, leader of the PLO.

archterrorist, genuinely but coolly positive from his supporters. His role has been to gather the shards of Palestine and give the whole a form and a cohesion it never had. Our case, he has seemed to us to be saying, is formulable; it can be represented in the forums of the world; it can stand up for itself on the field of battle. Second, he has introduced the various dispersed sectors of our society to each other: The camp-dweller has learned about the intellectual and vice versa, the millionaire about the poor student, the doctor about the patient, the worker about the banker. Third, and perhaps most important, he has postulated – I won't say fully articulated – a Palestinian idea, for which many of us have striven. Whereas historically Palestinian nationalism was thought of as a part of Arab nationalism whose misfortune it was to be confronted with and defeated by Jewish nationalism, leaving it in the attitude of a quasi-permanent Great Refusal – the politics of rejection – the force of Arafat's presiding character converted this sullen and disappointed residue into the idea of nonsectarian community – the politics of hope. No leader of any group in the Middle East so unambiguously sponsored so secular and genuinely liberating an idea: that Palestine might become the peacefully shared home of Arabs and Jews, and that no one group would have privileges over the other. And no leader has also seemed so catastrophically to be implicated in setbacks.

As I write, however, violence and snarling defensiveness have taken over. Sectarianism and the mentality of the security state rule. The Maronites want a state like the Jews, the Shi'ites want to dominate others as they have been dominated, many Israelis say that they want permanent dominion as Jews over the whole of the Holy Land. For our part, we are not closer to getting a Palestinian state. Too many of us feel that we have gained representation and media visibility at an exorbitant cost. We became known as hijackers and terrorists, and our much-vaunted 'armed struggle' landed us in the chambers of the United Nations, in debate for a full decade now, with dwindling attendance, and regrettably constant results. So are we now only a people of declarations, resolutions, statements, and are we therefore only creatures imprisoned by the affable international consensus telling us that, yes, we deserve self-determination, but that we must still be dependent on others, and still wait before we get it? The toll exacted from us by ourselves, by the Arabs, by the Israelis and Americans, by our Third World and socialist friends, has been too high, paid for in compromise, patience, changes of direction, and, some would say, corruption, accommodation and capitulation. Many ask whether the impurity of our current posture – unable to make either peace or war – might be cleansed by a reversion to the methods of South Lebanese Shi'ites, or of Algerian *mujahidin*.

New York. Nearly empty room at United Nations Day with the Palestinian People, November 29, 1983.

Tyre, South Lebanon, 1983. Building a house, Rashidyé camp. The tents have made way for huts, the huts for actual houses. Rebuilding follows destruction, exile becomes integration.

Atavism, I have thought. We cannot want the reign of an ayatollah, nor that of a relentless theoretician. But there is another way of interpreting our dissatisfaction. I do not think that we can see ourselves any longer the way we once did, when we caught glimpses of ourselves as a reflection, if not an imitation, of earlier, successful resistance movements. In the sixties and seventies it was not hard to see ourselves as somehow like the Algerians or the Cubans. Now, no models like these really work for us, and we have not yet come up with our own model. We have not fully assessed the complex and thoroughly mixed circumstances that bind us together as a people. There has not been time. The pressures are great, the task unprecedented for us. And it is not a job with a clear program and identifiable goal, as in fixing a car or conducting a survey.

Where should we start? First of all, I believe, we must become aware of the various forces in us that have made us a productive

124

people, rather than dwell on some Archimedean magic principle outside history or society. There is no lack of romance and eager energy, whether we locate it in life inside Palestine or in exile. Second, we should look at our young people, who, because they were born after 1948 without a country, do not embody a simple Palestinian destiny but normally stand at some point of convergence, however odd, between old and new, Arab and non-Arab, traditional and uncommon. Then the great questions become: What parts of our identity and history need to be preserved, and what parts abandoned, in the interests of a more workable dialectic of self and other? And can such knowledge actively and creatively connect our past and future, or will we fatalistically allow the workings of secular and sacred laws to guide our history?

Bir Zeit University, 1984.

4   Past and Future

Rafik Halabi, a Palestinian-Druze-Israeli who has worked as a reporter for Israeli radio and television covering the West Bank, wrote a book in 1982 about his experiences as an Arab Israeli, in particular his work as a journalist in the Occupied Territories. Halabi was fired for reporting the news in a way unfavorable to Israel, a predictable outcome of his position and opinions as a member of a disadvantaged and dispossessed minority. But that is not why his book, *The West Bank Story,* is so strangely interesting. Both Halabi and most of the Western critics who reviewed the book stress the fact that he writes from the viewpoint of a loyal Israeli: He served in the Israeli Defense Forces, he subscribes to Zionism, and he has no attachment whatever to the notion of a Palestinian state as a resolution to the Palestinian question or as the culmination of the processes of Palestinian nationalism. Yet despite authentic Israeli patriotism, virtually every page of his book, and certainly every significant episode in it, testifies to the discriminations against him and his people. Nothing in what he reports – whether it is the fact that as an Israeli Arab he is always suspected by Jews of being an alien and hence dangerous, or that his education in Hebrew schools totally ignored his own people's history, or that everywhere on the West Bank and Gaza since 1967 there has been a systematic policy of punishment, discrimination, and cruelty against the Palestinians – provides the reader with any grounds for understanding why Halabi persists in reiterating his faith in Israel's essential justice toward its non-Jewish citizens, who, he says without irony, 'have come to appreciate the benefits of democracy and the meaning of a life of freedom.' At most, he goes on to say, the non-Jew in a Jewish state faces 'a dilemma,' not a basic contradiction. Either Halabi is too deluded to take serious stock of his own evidence, for which he was, in effect, fired; or he is up to some elaborate rhetorical game, which I frankly cannot understand. The result is a book that runs on two completely different tracks. There is the narrative of his experiences,

Jerusalem, 1984. Mosque of Omar. Restoration work, mosaics.

127

which are all pretty depressing and hopeless. Then there is the fragmented text that attempts a reassuring commentary and a generally optimistic explanation of much that happens; in this other text Halabi seems to be glossing a quite different story from the one he actually narrates. He speaks, for example, of being an Israeli patriot, then admits that he 'never particularly liked Israeli society' for its treatment of him; a moment later he credits Israeli television for breaking down his 'prejudices on that score.'

Ramallah, 1984.

I thought of Halabi when I first saw Jean Mohr's remarkable photograph of an elderly Palestinian villager with a broken lens in his glasses. There is an irrepressible cheerfulness to the photograph as a whole, although the shattered lens still stands out with considerable force. A symbol, I said to myself, of some duality in our life that won't go away – refugees and terrorists, victims and victimizers, and so on. Having said that, however, I was dissatisfied with the concept behind the thought. If you look at the photograph honestly, you don't see anything about the man that suggests either pathos or weakness: He has a strong and gentle face; his smiling expression is obviously genuine (even if there is also a touch of wistfulness in it); and he radiates a welcoming, modestly assertive attitude which is very attractive. The blotch is on the lens, not in him; his other eye seems perfectly serviceable, and even if his vision is a little smudged, he can still see more or less everything there is to be seen.

What the photograph tells us is nothing so simple as a contradiction in the man's attitude to life. He has, after all, agreed to be photographed without either taking the glasses off or having them repaired. He has adjusted, and he seems relatively content

128

even though his son is in trouble. As I look at him I am bothered by how unresolved his cheerful resolution seems to be. I see one lens that is clear, another that is hopelessly impaired. Admittedly he does not need to depend very much on the broken one, since the intact lens seems sufficient, but no matter how clearly he sees (or is seen), there is always going to be some interference in vision, as well as some small disturbance for whoever looks at him. What is good and whole is never so good and whole as to overrule the bad, and vice versa. There is therefore some way in which this curiously balanced imbalance keeps bothering you every time you reexamine the photograph. The effect is very similar to the textual imbalance in Halabi's book, and this, one realizes, is an imbalance in consciousness, as if having taken on our Palestinian identity in the world we have not completely brought into harmony the wildness and disorganization of our history with our declared and apparently coherent political, social, and cultural personality.

Are we interested in liberation? Are we about independence? There is no great episode in our history that establishes imperatives for our future course, partly because our past is still ragged, discredited, and unassimilated, partly because we endure the difficulties of dispersion without being forced (or able) to struggle to change our circumstances. We have no dominant theory of Palestinian culture, history, society; we cannot rely on one central image (exodus, holocaust, long march); there is no completely coherent discourse adequate to us, and I doubt whether at this point, if someone could fashion such a discourse, we could be adequate for it. Miscellaneous, the spaces here and there in our midst include but do not comprehend the past; they represent building without overall purpose, around an uncharted and only partially surveyed territory. Without a center. Atonal.

Nablus, 1979. The cemetery at the center of the city.

129

Perhaps I am only describing *my* inability to order things coherently, sequentially, logically, and perhaps the difficulties of resolution I have discerned in Halabi's book and in the old man with broken glasses are mine, not theirs. I write at a distance. I haven't experienced the ravages. If I had, possibly there would be no problem in finding a direct and simple narrative to tell the tale of our history. When I let myself go and feel as if everything in the Palestinian situation flows directly from one original trauma, I can then see a pattern emerging inexorably, as intertwined and as recountable as any other sequential tale of misfortune. What I have found is that if you seize on all the evidence that appears intermittently – another massacre, one more betrayal, a damaging defeat – you can easily construct the plot of a logically unfolding conspiracy against us. Like all paranoid constructions, this one could add up to a whole thing ('could' is a conditional word) if the 'normal' world cooperated. But our narratives in general have little official or recognized status; few people have given us the privilege even of having a narrative, much less of publicizing it; as outlaws we are always so censored and interdicted that we seem able only to get occasional messages through to an indifferent outside world. In any case, I can't sustain the paranoid view for long.

Certain things, however, do seem to me to be seriously incontrovertible. One is that, historically, we have been regarded as a population that is essentially disposable, the subject people or inferior race of classical imperialism. We have been transported, dislocated, and dispossessed according to the same principle: Palestinians are not a coherent national group. (One of the saddest of Kanafani's tales, 'The Land of Sad Oranges,' embodies this fate in the peregrinations of a Jaffa family; its poignancy is almost unmatched in our literature.) Thus it is possible to see us as radically focused outward, toward a center of authority we do not ourselves provide. It is as if we have internalized the views of an outside authority, participated in *its* schemes. Sometimes this focus is the U.N.; at others it is Arab nationalism and one or another Arab state or leader; and at still others we are held together by an idea of liberation. Most of the time, however, we are in the grip of Israeli power.

We've taken on the de-centered role. The Palestinian is very much a person in transit: Suitcase or bundle of possessions in hand, each family vacates territory left behind for others, even as new boundaries are traversed, new opportunities created, new realities set up. It could even be argued that we are too mobile and too adaptable. Is this why we did not prevent our own exodus in 1948? In the end we can't give ourselves too much credit for being forced out by terror, instead of standing fast, organizing, fighting; the excuse that we did not know that an irrevocable loss would result

June, 1967. Release of Palestinian civilians by Israeli authorities.

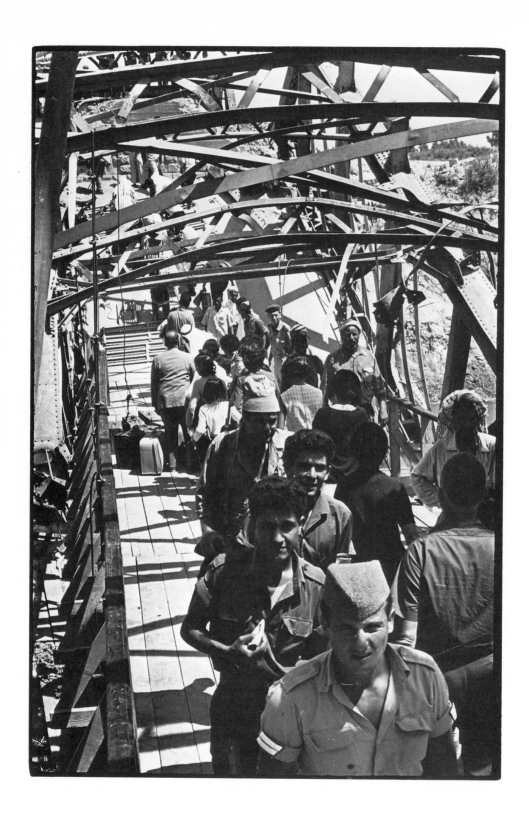

*Allenby Bridge, 1967.
Palestinian exodus after
the June War.*

from our departure certainly does not help now, especially since it has been used since 1967 to justify the panicked flight of Palestinians who lost their property for the second time. My aunt Nabiha used to mutter frequently about the great houses that were built in Ramallah and Jerusalem in the fifties and sixties: Don't they have any idea, she would say, that they're going to lose them? Why do they build with such grandeur and ostentation? Why don't they plan in some way for the difficulties ahead? Her views were that we weren't mobilized, committed, serious enough, that we didn't use our will enough to get back our original homes with a force that would be more tenacious than 'theirs.'

A second incontrovertible fact is that the alliance between Zionism and the United States ultimately caused our dispossession, and prolongs it to this day. In his recently published study *Palestine 1948: L'Expulsion,* Elie Sanbar argues that this alliance derived from the historical processes of capitalism. Ben-Gurion, he says, knew what he was doing when he joined the movement to the United States. Doubtless, as Sanbar shows, the desire to create a postwar society from scratch in an outlying and preferably hostile region of the world was appealing to U.S. planners, for whom the capitalist trajectory was legitimized *ab origine* by the mythos of a miraculous birth followed by fabulous prosperity. And it has always struck me as true that the affinity between Zionist and American campaigns to devastate native inhabitants of a land decreed to be empty *par hypothèse,* as Sanbar has it, was profound and compelling. In the mind of America, Israel has occupied a privileged place, so privileged as to be the subject of a recent book – *Israel in the Mind of America* – which presents the relationship between the two countries in the form of an idyll that contains hardly any references to the directly consequent and concrete deprivations of Palestinian life. It is as if Palestine had been a nondescript locale in the process of being evacuated by faceless natives, *until* Americans thought better of it and filled it with deserving Zionists. Any Palestinian who wishes to understand the peculiar miseries of his or her situation today must reckon with an almost total official American opposition to us as a people, as a society, as a cause. You can scarcely imagine what it means to a Palestinian to watch one American political, cultural, or religious figure after another in an endless series declaring his or her allegiance to Israel, while the government dispenses astronomical funds in aid to Israel and issues attacks on Palestinian terrorism with numbing repetition – all occurring simultaneously with the equally long list of outrages committed against us, the tortures, the killings, the invasions, and, above all, the prohibition of our political identity and the systematic dispossession of our people. Not only do we suffer directly at the hands of Israel and America, but the *truth* of our suffering and the

133

worth of our cause are almost totally negated by the most powerful public relations apparatus (or, as it is euphemistically called in Hebrew, *hasbara*: 'information' for the outside world) ever invented. I say 'almost totally' because since 1982, a series of public opinion polls conducted for Arab-American scholars (Fouad Moughrabi and Elia Zureik principally) by the major American polling agencies have shown conclusively that U.S. government policy is considerably at odds with U.S. public opinion, which in fact *favors* a Palestinian state and is generally much less sympathetic to Israeli policy than is commonly supposed. But there is no getting around the horrific coincidences between Israeli and American policies, especially in the last ten years; and to the extent that Israel remains tied to the United States in as many ways as it is tied at present, official America is our enemy. An irresistible truth, which every American Zionist honestly would have no other way.

A third fact is that in the world system today there is no method, no way, no perspective that gives us an existence as a people independent of, and to some small degree transcending, the very events and factors that have reduced us to our present pass. I can put this more starkly. There has been no misfortune worse for us than that we are ineluctably viewed as the enemies of the Jews. No moral and political fate worse, none at all, I think: no worse, there is none. With so much discussion recently of the Holocaust, I am centrally aware of the fact of the destruction of European Jews, an abomination which nevertheless I find hard to consider separately; there is always the connection made between Israel and the Holocaust, how one makes restitution for the other. I find myself saying that a generation later the Holocaust has victimized us too, but without the terrifying grandeur and sacrilegious horror of what it did to the Jews. Seen from the perspective provided by the Holocaust, we are as inconsequential as children on a playground; and yet – one more twist in the reductive spiral – even at play we cannot be enjoyed or looked at simply as that, as children playing games that signify little. Just by virtue of where we stand, every playground is seen as a 'breeding ground for terrorists,' every pastime a 'secret plan for the destruction of Israel,' as if our own destruction was not a great deal more probable. Something either pernicious or negligible can be attributed to us, no matter what we do, wherever we are, however we think or act.

The gross outlines of our victimization do not, at this late moment in our history of conflict with Zionists, interest and obsess me as much as the symptoms, the telling details, the significant side issues, which we have often overlooked through that unresolved attitude to life that characterizes everything we do. If we look closely it is easy enough to see that the violence against us goes on, getting at every small corner of our lives, intervening and establishing an

Jarash camp, near Irbid, 1983. Gymnastic demonstration for visitors.

enemy presence wherever we thought we were safest. The main dishes of Palestinian cuisine, for instance, have become staples of the Israeli diet: *Tabooleh* appears on some restaurant menus as 'kibbutz salad.' The standard Hebrew method for transliterating Arabic words and names has now completely taken over the American press; this enrages me to an absurd degree. It used to be the case that the Arabic guttural *h* would be rendered in English as *h*. Ever since 1982 the *New York Times*, among others, has changed it to *kh*, which corresponds to the nearest Hebrew equivalent. Thus the largest refugee camp in Lebanon, Ein el-Hilwé, has been

135

transformed into *Ein el-Khilwé,* an unintentional pun. *Hilwé* means 'sweet,' *Ein el-Hilwé,* 'sweet spring'; *Ein el-Khilwé,* on the other hand, means something close to 'a spring in the empty place.' In the new spelling, I see an allusion to the mass graves in the regularly razed and not always rebuilt camp, and I also register the thought that Israel has indeed emptied the camp of its Palestinian wellsprings. Conversely, until recently the *kh* letter in Arabic was always transliterated as *kh,* corresponding in pronunciation to the *ch* in *Loch.* Now it has been changed routinely to *h,* so that *Karim Khalaf* has become *Karim Halaf.* Trivial.

How much trivial malice can we bear? Acre and Jaffa were after all once major Palestinian cities rich in Arab traditions as well as a host of European associations. Trevor-Roper is Lord Dacre, a Crusader title. I know many natives of these two coastal cities with excruciatingly nostalgic recollections of their homes, their adolescent pastimes, their family life and communal pleasures all left behind. But they do exist, as Proust says all memory exists, with a solidity and durability that can be recaptured now and again. Proust did not live long enough to say that memory has become almost entirely official, conflated – as John Berger puts it – with

Acre, 1979. From the walls of the old port, young Palestinians jump and dive into the sea.

History. And History, we all know, exists only for historians, who are accredited with responsibility for the topic in the places where power and respectability reside. Some weeks ago I walked past a colleague's office and noted an announcement for a lecture. (This colleague regularly posts things on his office door. All of them are announcements for good causes – antiapartheid, antinuclear, anti-intervention in Nicaragua, profeminist – and yet none is ever for Palestinians. The Middle East is politely avoided.) One word of the title of the lecture caught my eye almost violently: 'Crusader Acre: Profile of a Medieval City in the Levant.' It was 'Acre,' of course, that I saw first. Then, almost too depressingly for words, there followed what I had come to expect: The lecturer was an Israeli, from the Hebrew University. Making the only response I could and a pathetic one at that, I looked around to make sure no one could see me, then took down the little poster, which in jumping from Arab Acre to the Levant, to medieval times, to Israel greatly annoyed me. I folded it up, and have carried it around in my briefcase for six weeks.

During and after Ariel Sharon's libel suit against *Time* in New York, the newspapers were full of opinions about his innocence or guilt, the meaning of the suit for American libel law, the portent of

137

the verdict for Jewish conscience, and so forth. The day after the
verdict was pronounced, the *New York Times,* for example, carried
four op-ed pieces, not one of them by a Palestinian, all of them
discussing Sharon as if he were just another average person or civil
case. Never did it occur to any of the commentators that in a true
sense the trial concerned not only the fine points of a civil suit, or the
victims of the massacres, but the Palestinian experience as a whole,
of which the massacres were a part. Only on rare occasions, when
some relief from the procession of 'terrorists' and 'fanatics' is
needed, is an 'Arab' (we are all generically the same) trotted out to
say something – inevitably in a voice made to seem liberal or
moderate, totally unthreatening, uniformly out of touch with our
realities.

I think they are all of a piece, these tiny offenses against the
scattered truth of our lives. Israel means less to me as a real place
than as a force whose imponderable power and purpose weaves
disparity and contradictions into a figure in the carpet. Maybe the
carpet is only mine, and maybe it is entirely my paranoia that
convinces me that even when we hear terrorism discussed as a
global phenomenon, as it is every day, I am right to think that the

implication of Palestinian involvement always lurks between the lines, and that Israel slides into place on the good side. Think of the Jonathan Institute in Washington, devoted to the memory of Jonathan Netanyahu, hero of Entebbe, Israeli fighter against *all* terrorism.

Similarly, whereas Nuremberg is invoked as a touchstone for judging war practices in, say, Vietnam, it is quickly withdrawn when Israel is concerned. A colleague who was centrally involved in Nuremberg called me out of the blue during the 1982 invasion. A commission had been set up to investigate Israeli war crimes, he said, and he was going to join it; but he refused to say anything more. Sean MacBride, the Nobel Prize winner and founder of Amnesty International, in the meantime did his inquiry with a group of distinguished jurists; their book, *Israel in Lebanon,* came out in England, but it was never published in the United States. My colleague disappeared thereafter, only to reappear whenever there was an occasion for reminiscences, ceremonies, ritual tokens of the horrors condemned at Nuremberg.

No tribunal for us. We are the criminals. We are not victims at all. Arab Jaffa is at best a symbolic interruption of a distant vista.

Jaffa, 1979. From the old city, a glimpse of the new city.

What I have been saying is that we ourselves provide not enough of a presence to force the untidiness of life into a coherent pattern of our own making. At best, to judge simply from my case, we can read ourselves against another people's pattern, but since it is not ours – even though we are its designated enemy – we emerge as its effects, its errata, its counternarratives. Whenever we try to narrate ourselves, we appear as dislocations in *their* discourse.

They speak the language of power, after all, and as their pronouncements pour forth, especially in the United States, the one country on whom Israel depends above all others, you realize – I realize – the extraordinary dangers of that sense of power. The heads of various U.S. Jewish organizations, for example, possess astonishing political clout. They have the ability to hurt the careers of people who have something positive to say about Palestinians: Vanessa Redgrave, Paul Findley, Pete McCloskey, even Charles Percy, and too many lesser-known people to list here. On February 25, 1985, the head of the American Israel Public Affairs Committee (AIPAC) reported that at present we have 'the most pro-Israel Congress in history,' and what he means is that anything Israel wants it will get. At an instant, seventy or eighty senators can be launched into action, attacking the administration or the President for daring to think of selling arms for cash to an Arab country, or for daring to criticize Israel in some way or another. In the years since 1982, three or four books have been published by Bnai Brith, AIPAC, and others, identifying pro-Arab, pro-Palestinian groups in narrative, as well as encyclopedic, form. This sort of group portrait, by the way, is something we have never done for ourselves; now it has been done for us.

In addition, there are prominent American magazines whose officially declared policy is not to print criticism of Israel, or to do so only from a Zionist perspective; others insist that all writing about Israel be done by Jews, or by well-known non-Jewish supporters of Israel. More: There is now a barely contained hostility between the Israeli lobby in the United States and the U.S. media, a hostility that has not prevented the lobbyists from packing the media with pro-Israel material and attacking it in the tone of a nasty schoolmaster when it fails to follow the party line, or dares to report the Palestinians as a people rather than as terrorists, or presumes to suggest that Israel's ironfisted policies are anything other than highly civilized. (Since it is commonly thought that the British, French, Italian, Spanish, and German media are all pro-Arab, they've simply been written off.)

In all this vigilante propaganda, there is something desperate, something truly horrendous in the price it exacts from its adherents. If you need a virtual thought police to champion a cause, something is wrong. I do not want the same thing for us, and in fact I do not know any Palestinian who does. If our lesser status as the victims of a major Victim has any consolation, it is that from our relatively humble vantage point we can see our adversaries going through the enormously complicated procedures to get around us or pretend we are not there. Take the case of a political philosopher who argued that Israel was the Zionist dream fulfilled. For such a theory, the presence of a simple Palestinian vendor – non-Jewish, clearly a second-class citizen – is a serious flaw, and so the theory must be hedged with various protections that put the Palestinian out of bounds, render him marginal. Why? Because the Palestinian, who may seem only picturesque to most people, is a reminder that before the state of Israel existed there were natives in Palestine; rather than acknowledge that Israel rules a colonial population, the philosopher must now go back over his own earlier arguments against colonialism, discover merits in the colonizing community, and then say that since colonialism is, after all, practiced by a community of people with undeniable moral rights, it cannot be so bad. The street vendor, however, plies the street, hawks his wares, and goes on as he was. The arguments do not touch him.

Jerusalem, 1984.
Water-seller.

Or take the American reaction to the militant Palestinian students in the Occupied Territories. These students have quite literally become the vanguard of struggle against the occupation, but they have paid a steep price in arrests, houses demolished, schools and universities closed. If this were happening almost anywhere else, there would be a solid phalanx of professors protesting the infringements on academic freedom. With the exception of the usual intrepid few, the opposite has been the case. I will never forget the visit to Columbia University some years ago of an Orientalist from an Israeli university who happened also to be an Occupation official (no one seemed to bother about *that* coincidence). A few small meetings were set up with him, and for reasons I still do not know, I was invited to one. Although I left after a few minutes, I was aghast at the deference with which he was treated by liberal academics whose attitude toward counterpart American officials (the war in Vietnam was still in progress) was justifiably hostile. One of my colleagues at the meeting then remarked on the miracle – I think that was the word used – of Israel's 'liberal' occupation. How do you do it, he asked him, and how do you manage to keep your sense of perspective?

Since that time, of course, the situation has worsened considerably. And still, it is next to impossible to interest most American intellectuals in joining the effort to apply sustained pressure on the Israeli government to lift the censorship on books, magazines, and curricula, or to stop a policy of shutting down entire universities for months on end whenever a festival of Palestinian culture appears to threaten Israeli security. That in addition there is a system of virtual apartheid, in which the rights of Arabs and Jews are legislatively unequal and Arab students are prescriptively inferior, gets no recognition from signers of manifestos and petitions about every other place in the world. Even the collaboration between Israel and South Africa, or between Israel and nearly every repressive right-wing regime in the Third World, from Central and South America to Africa to the Far East, is regularly ignored, or suppressed. I once asked a well-known academic friend why he did not accept an invitation to give a lecture at Bir Zeit while he was in Israel. He said, as if it were unnecessary to explain further, that the invitation on behalf of Bir Zeit had come from a group of British 'friends' of the university (an association whose members include such distinguished scholars as Joseph Needham, Michael Atiyah, and Raymond Williams), who, this important academician said, constituted an Arab front group. I must say that I had nothing by way of rejoinder, so effective in stopping my persuasive powers was the disqualifying force of the phrase 'Arab front group.'

To look at the perhaps plodding efforts of a group of Islamic

Bir Zeit, 1984. Two students in conversation between classes, on the terrace of the university.

*Jerusalem, 1984,
Koranic studies within the
walls of the Mosque of
Omar.*

school students in Jerusalem is therefore to feel some satisfaction at
how their unexceptional attention to the Koran – I speak from an
essentially non-religious viewpoint – furnishes a counterweight to
all the sophisticated methods employed to wish them away. I do not
by any means refer to the so-called Islamic resurgence, which is
what every resistance to Israel is converted to these days (as if 'the
Shi'ite fundamentalists' of South Lebanon, or 'the Arab terrorists'
on the West Bank, did not have the same antioccupation drive as
any other *Maquis* in history). What I do mean, however, is that the
local attentions of Palestinians – to their work, families, teachers,
and friends – are in fact so many potential breaks in the seamless
text, the unendingly unbroken narrative of U.S./Israeli power.

144

*Bir Zeit University, 1984.
Chemistry laboratory.*

*Amman, 1984. Hospital of
the University of Jordan.
Dr. Najwa Khoury
Boulus, a pediatrician in
consultation.*

Far from being cheerful nonentities at work on some small project
nowhere in particular, we represent a concrete force whose
dispersed and uncentralized power even we cannot easily discern.
But it gives what we do a fragmented dignity. A whole series of
Mohr's photographs of Palestinians at work or at study, for
example, reveals an intensity and seriousness at odds with the
episodic and storyless nature of the photographs. Dressmakers in
the Baqa'a camp in Amman; a chemistry lab at Bir Zeit University;
two students doing an experiment, perhaps, next door to a group in
class; a doctor with a child and her mother in an Amman University
clinic. These are quiet but powerful photographs whose common
theme is the communication of attention and alertness. Mohr's style
is transparent: He enables us to see Palestinians in the process of
sustaining themselves, perhaps even of re-presenting themselves
outside the debilitating confinements of their real situation with an
immediacy that is surprisingly strong.

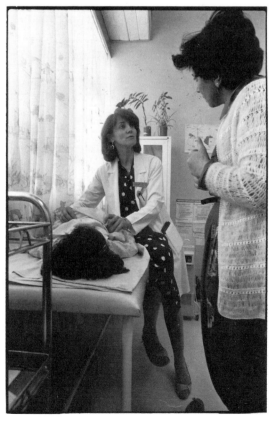

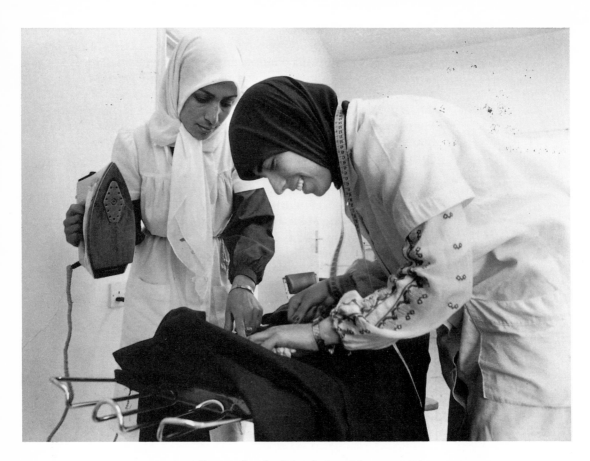

Except for the Islamic headdresses of the two young women, nothing in these photographs is freighted with the kind of history that has brought these Palestinians – refugee and inhabitant of Palestine still, worker and student, doctor and technician – to their present pass. What you see in each is a person concentrating on his or her situation, working out of it, generating a local momentum that can be satisfying despite the precarious circumstances that we assume encompass the scene. What could seem depressing about something as self-enclosed and limited as these people's work is nevertheless an entirely successful tactical solution to a predicament for which no clear strategy is available for the moment.

Small-mindedness? The limited efforts of a limited people? I do not believe so. Mohr's photographs here are evidence of a Palestinian ecology that is neither symbolic nor representative in some hokey nationalist way; rather, we are presented addressing our world as a secular place, without nostalgia for a lost transcendance. Here are people doing their utmost to address the everyday material world with purpose and grit. Consider these

Amman, 1984. Baqa'a camp, dressmakers.

146

photographs, then, not as evidence of triviality, but as scenes of people who, in having left behind some untellable trauma, some offstage catastrophe (*nakba*), now respond directly to the task at hand with an unmistakable determination that I have come to recognize as irreducibly Palestinian.

More needs to be said about this. All across the Arab world there is a mixture of cultural styles that characterizes rapid development: Modern Western modes of dress, activity, and architecture are superimposed on traditional settings and ways of being. The commonest symbol of this process is to be found in the typical photographs of an old city across which is laid a grid of radio and television antennae. What we get is a site of intensity that makes reference to two traditions, one native, the other foreign or Western, held in a kind of awkward check by each other. You are left to compute the various gains and losses resulting from this kind of balance, and you are also led to think of two worlds in sustained tension. A more just representation of how the mixture of elements actually occurs and is experienced in modern Arab life is found, I think, in photographs of traditional sites whose undeniable

Jerusalem, 1979. A forest of television antennae.

Jerusalem, 1984. The Mosque of Omar.

148

centrality stands out, and draws in, by subordinating, the intruding symbols of metropolitan modernity. This is the slower and more delicate way everyone absorbs and reorients the new according to the still redoubtable force of the old and habitual.

Yet both of these perspectives do not account adequately for the local quality of Palestinian existence, which has developed since 1948. Dispossession and dispersion have meant a fundamental discrepancy between 'us' and wherever each of us now happens to be. Each of us bears the loss of place and of history acutely, the given we share at the root of our various lives. There is no way for us to feel the accumulations of our past except as a gap, an apparently unchanging abyss separating us from the national fulfillment we have not yet been able to attain. As internal exiles in Israel, as detainees on the West Bank or Gaza without sovereignty over land, as refugees and itinerant exiles, we are not likely to recuperate our loss of a settled national existence. The tie between us and our past was not only severed in 1948; it is periodically and ritually resevered in the sustained war upon our national peoplehood by Israel. And whenever we have set up an alternative national existence – in Jordan and in Lebanon – that too has been destroyed. The meaning of Israeli troops carting off our archives from Beirut in September 1982 was lost on no one.

The severity and rigor of this series of difficult truths is, I believe, absorbed into our notion of the present. What existed in the past for

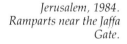

Jerusalem, 1984. Ramparts near the Jaffa Gate.

us – the *there* of our memories – is still there, but because it is irredeemable and inaccessible, it has acquired the complex, impersonal texture of an ancient wall: you can neither have it, nor

149

penetrate it. Yet, curiously, this aspect of the past can be reinscribed in the present. It does affect our sense of where and how each of us is now. You learn a certain kind of caring for and attention to your immediate situation if you know that in time it too can become the place you will have lost forever, the place whose identity is retained only in the repeated experience of staying and then moving on. Homecoming is out of the question. You learn to transform the mechanics of loss into a constantly postponed metaphysics of return. Mahmoud Darwish:

> But I am the exile.
> Seal me with your eyes.
> Take me wherever you are –
> Take me whatever you are.
> Restore to me the color of face
> And the warmth of body
> The light of heart and eye,
> The salt of bread and rhythm,
> The taste of earth . . . The Mother land.
> Shield me with your eyes.
> Take me as a relic from the mansion of sorrows.
> Take me as a verse from any tragedy;
> Take me as a toy, a brick from the house
> So that our children will remember to return.

A part of something is for the foreseeable future going to be better than all of it. Fragments over wholes. Restless nomadic activity over the settlements of held territory. Criticism over resignation. The Palestinian as self-consciousness in a barren plain of investments and consumer appetites. The heroism of anger over the begging-bowl, limited independence over the status of clients. Attention, alertness, focus. To do as others do, but somehow to stand apart. To tell your story in pieces, *as it is.*

And all of this alongside and intervening in a closed orbit of Jewish exile and a recuperated, much-celebrated patriotism of which Israel is the emblem. Better our wanderings, I sometimes think, than the horrid clanging shutters of their return. The open secular element, and not the symmetry of redemption.

PAST AND FUTURE   Our past marches before me in those dreary funeral processions of old women, anonymous stragglers, and listless boys looking on. Black is the distinctive color here – priestly robes, women's dresses, men's suits, all of them suggesting a generalized death accompanied by extravagant lunches, religious mummies, religious

Jerusalem, 1979.
Pilgrims, Via Dolorosa.

151

Jerusalem, 1979. Priests, Via Dolorosa.

pilgrimages, devalued rituals. We are drenched in religion, only a tiny corner of which we see, only a small part of which concerns us. What a fate for Palestine: to have attracted the religious imagination and the dramas of the apocalypse not just once, but three times: Judaism, Christianity, Islam, the latter the most austere, least known, and most abominated. Lift off the veneer of religious cant – which speaks of the 'best and noblest in the Judaic, Christian, or Muslim tradition,' in perfectly interchangeable phrases – and a seething cauldron of outrageous fables is revealed, seething with several bestiaries, streams of blood, and innumerable corpses.

And however readily one may forgive a Dante, or a Ma'arri, or even a renegade-heretic Sabbatai Zvi for their appropriations of the Palestinian aura, it is difficult for me to accept the abominations visited on the soil of Palestine and its hapless people by the contemporary fundamentalists – Christian, Jewish, and Muslim as well. When you hear the prattlings of Jerry Falwell or any of his born-again crew, all of them staunch supporters of Israel, you are aghast at the utter madness of what they believe, particularly when you hear about their special treatment during visits to Israel – expert

152

tour guides to show them around; leading Israeli government officials to address them. According to the scenario proposed by these fundamentalist Christians, Russia and Israel – Gog and Magog – will have an apocalyptic final battle, which Russia will win, until Jesus intervenes (but not soon enough to prevent the death of all Jews; Arabs don't seem to figure in it at all). In the meantime, the true Christians will be suspended over Israel, above the battle, in Raptures, and after the fighting is over Jesus will restore them to Jerusalem, from which they will rule the world.

As for the Jewish fundamentalists of the Third Temple Movement, or the zealots of Gush Emunim and their cohorts in the Tehiya party, the scavenging power of these fanatics complements the insanities of their Christian counterparts. Not for nothing then has the Islamic chorus risen in response, like a specter in one of Blake's visions or Shelley's late apocalyptic poems, intended to make you lose the thread of argument and grasp only the terrifyingly vague, blood-dripping imagery. *Jihad* and Islamic law have the reactive force to stimulate young men and women for such suicidal struggle as the politics of secular liberation has never dreamed of.

Hebron, 1979.
Mosque of Abraham.

It is this Dionysiac realm that dominates our world now, although the press seems fascinated disproportionately by its Islamic manifestations. Whether these deranged imaginings are spillovers from the sectarian madness that has torn Lebanon apart, or residues left behind by the East-West confrontation, or vestiges welling up from the coarse millennarian passions of the Crusades, the Inquisition, and the Reformation, I do not know. I do know that there seems to be an absolute discontinuity between all that and the dry Protestant atmosphere in which I was raised. Those interminable pious Sundays of my childhood, with their triadic succession of English, American, and Arabic services we regularly attended, the heavy midday meal, and the prohibition of anything more pleasurable than an early afternoon BBC program on opera – I feel for all that a nostalgia stimulated and made positively acute by Jean Mohr's account of his trip to Amman, where somehow he fell in with the Anglican community I left behind long ago, who had re-created the subdued and arid atmosphere of Jerusalem of the thirties and forties. I remember also the stubborn but gentle and ineffective protests of my grandmother, who in her absolute adherence to Protestantism refused to drink even a drop of wine from the communion chalice. She was a literalist when it came to the Bible – it was God's word – but for her, as for us as children, it was the story that mattered, the exchanges between Moses and Pharaoh, Joseph and Potiphar's wife, Jesus and Pilate, exchanges that she led up to carefully and then rendered with a burning fidelity to the unadorned truth of how people – not plumed saints or imaginary heroes – could stand up for what they took to be right and

Amman, 1984. Annual guest night at Ahliyah Girls' School. After the entertainment, visitors and parents greet the Anglican bishop, Ilya Khoury.

154

just. Each of the narrations of the climactic scenes she did so well would invariably begin with the homely admonition 'Now look here,' and indeed we could look and be able to see plain men and women engaged in telling and speaking, exactly as we told and spoke.

All of this has disappeared in the swirl of noisy chiliastic visions that are actually visionless with regard to the secular world of men and women in society. Better to suffer the mundane, humdrum search of the individual tourist in the Holy Land, beset with

Jerusalem, 1979. Tourist pilgrims in the Holy Sepulcher.

155

problems of currency exchange and language, than the grand certainties of the overbearing priest, imam, or rabbi. But those religious figures have become fixtures of the land of Palestine. The question becomes how to get past them or, more to the point, how to make proper use of them without letting them dislodge us completely. There is a short story by Tawfik Zayyad about a dog, Sammur, that serves as a metaphor of our position lost at the center of an immensely turbulent storm. When British troops invade the village of Maqeibleh, Sammur turns on the military (who could just as well be clerics); the British are followed by Arab troops, and then in turn by Zionist soldiers, and the dog is hostile to them all. But at least he gets to go back to his village to die at home, whereas his master's family is dispossessed and can never return.

Sanctuary of Samuel near Jerusalem, 1979. A priest looks toward Ramallah.

All through the months of looking at Jean Mohr's photographs and writing this book I have been haunted by two of Yeats's poems, 'Leda and the Swan,' and 'Among School Children,' poems whose familiarity and extraordinary staying power have the capacity over time to take on an unexpected set of references. In 1972 and 1973 I spent a sabbatical year in Beirut and was visited there by my Columbia colleague and close friend, Fred Dupee. One of the first things he noticed when he entered our house in Beirut was a copy of Yeats's *Collected Poems,* which I had brought along with me. 'There's your Yeats,' he said. 'Funny, but nice to see him here.' Indeed Yeats, for all his Irish and Greek allusions, wrote himself frequently into my thoughts and actions in those early years of the Palestinian renaissance after 1967. It was a natural association, given Yeats's frequent method of focusing on distant historical moments and then letting them gather strands of contemporary allusion into a new and often unexpected structure of feeling.

Such a structure gradually became apparent to me a short time later, when I read a brilliant dissertation by Hanan Mikhail Ashrawi, a young Palestinian lecturer in English at Bir Zeit University. Hanan Ashrawi's thesis concerned the impact of occupation on the sensibility of Palestinian writers, and it brought to mind the parallel between occupation – the forceful and brutal intervention in the lives of ordinary people by an outside force – and the story of Leda and Zeus. Yeats's last stanza:

> Being so caught up,
> So mastered by the brute blood of the air,
> Did she put on his knowledge with his power
> Before the indifferent beak could let her drop?

In such a situation, Ashrawi argued, the writer necessarily has several imperatives to respond to, chief among them being the raising of national consciousness, the carefully realistic rendering of particular situations, and perhaps less important, the discovery of adequate norms of aesthetic performance. She concludes by saying that Palestinian writers cannot be underestimated for what they have done: They have produced a defiant and progressive body of literature, they have borne witness to the trials of occupation, and they have urged their readers to a sense of solidarity and national unity. Nevertheless, Ashrawi's real point goes further than that. Much of what writers under occupation have written is often not good, she shows, simply because it has been trying to do too many urgent things all at once. What we need, she says, is a sense of responsibility in critics and writers alike, so that weak literature will not be excused just because it is Palestinian (and hence of national significance) or because it has understandably neglected exigencies of style and form for the pressures of politics.

*Paris, 1984. Mahmoud
Darwish, national
Palestinian poet.*

    Hanan Ashrawi's critical thesis is a sign of something important, if not easily visible, in the present Palestinian situation. I have no doubt that the vast majority of our people are now thoroughly sick of the misfortunes that have befallen us partly through our own fault, partly because of who our dispossessors are, and partly because our cause has a singular ineffectuality to it, capable neither of sufficiently mobilizing our friends, nor of overcoming our enemies. On the other hand, I have never met a Palestinian who is tired enough of being Palestinian to give up entirely. Most of us still rally to our cause, even though a mixture of skepticism and fatigue (after all, how long can you go on losing?) breaks in whenever a new campaign gets under way. Thus we are left with yearnings for a future settlement that are both imprecise and strong, imprecise as to how or when the process will occur, strong in that every one of us knows that a settlement between us and Israel must come about if we are to survive as a nation. There is a notable stubbornness to these feelings that must not be discounted. It derives from a sense of accumulated Palestinian history that is at once too public and too engraved in our current situation to be rolled back or ignored. Today, there are very few of us who can avoid the fate of every Palestinian, which is both to be *there*, and yet not to be accounted for politically. In addition, we have, as a nation, grown into and begun to express in our politics and literature the love of Palestine, which gets perhaps its first major statement in al-Muqadasi, the tenth-century Arab-Palestinian geographer. Palestine, he says, 'unites the joys of this world and of the other; whoever is of this world and aspires to the other, will in Palestine be able to feel the appeal of that other world; and whoever is of the other world will find in Palestine all the good of which this world is capable.'

Thus our need for a new consciousness, as Hanan Ashrawi reminds us in the concluding lines of her dissertation, is that of a people whose national experience belongs, with that of the Armenians, the Jews, the Irish, the Cypriots, the American blacks, the Poles, the American Indians, at those terrifying frontiers where the existence and disappearance of peoples fade into each other, where resistance is a necessity, but where there is also sometimes a growing realization of the need for an unusual and, to some degree, an unprecedented knowledge. For, having had the experience of limits, we are thrown back on ourselves in this period of political indecisiveness and forced to raise the issues of whether we have learned what it is that has brought us this fate (perhaps *not* the worst in history), whether there is anything we can do to change it, and whether, based on the realities of our past, we can responsibly articulate a sense of the future to which all of us can adhere and aspire. Can we 'put on' knowledge adequate to the power that has entered and dislocated our lives so unalterably in this century? Can we see what we are, have we really *seen* what we have seen?

It is difficult to go further than posing the questions in this tentative form. Too many details of our disparate and, it often seems, hopelessly scattered existence bombard me as I try to order my thoughts into sequential prose. At best, I feel about these various Palestinian existences that they form a counterpoint (if not a cacophony) of multiple, almost desperate dramas, which each of us

Paris, 1984. Jabra Ibrahim Jabra, novelist, poet, translator.

159

is aware of as occurring simultaneously with his or her own. Now, for example, the air here is full of the PLO-Jordanian peace initiative. Yet the Palestinian press and word of mouth bring accounts of new expropriations, collective punishments and detention centers (our geographical consciousness is regularly invaded by the names of prisons like Ansar, Neve Terza, and Atlit, where Israeli soldiers, in their own words, 'abuse and humiliate the men,' and where torture, beatings, and death occur with alarming frequency), of the horrifically unsanitary conditions in Sabra and Shatila (sympathetic Western eyewitnesses have given some especially harrowing descriptions of uncontrollable sewage and disease in the Beirut Palestinian refugee camps), of the difficulties facing Palestinian education throughout the Arab world since 1982. These only begin to cover the degree to which our collective politics, consolidated and centralized in Beirut until 1982, have become unraveled, with no national authority sufficiently strong to hold us together.

There has been no diminishment in the pressures on us. In the West we, the weakest by far of all the parties to the Arab-Israeli conflict, are cast in the role of biggest villain, obstacle to peace, intransigent and immoderate in our demands. Because we are weak, the largest concessions are demanded of us in advance. Thus the Americans refuse to speak with our representatives because in 1975 Israel and Henry Kissinger inserted a clause in the Sinai II agreement that the United States would not deal with the PLO *unless* we met conditions designed in effect to eliminate ourselves – a formula breathtaking in its arrogance, since it imposes unheard-of conditions on us. (What, in international diplomacy, does it mean to 'recognize the existence and legitimacy' of a state? Since when can one party decide who represents its enemies? Why are we required to accept U.N. resolutions, like 242, that do not even refer to us?) Victims of the destruction of our society, dispossessed ever since, regularly the target of genocidal intentions, we are expected meekly not to resist; in addition, we are lectured on the need to renounce violence, to stop insisting on designating our own representatives, to give up our wish to have an independent state of our own, to respond to American demands for peace. Meanwhile America supplies our enemy with everything and refuses to condemn such flagrantly illegal measures by Israel against us as the use of U.S. weapons, including cluster bombs, to invade Lebanon and bomb civilians in the camps; the detention of thousands of Palestinians without giving them prisoner-of-war status; the use of ironfisted policies that match, blow by blow, practices against Yugoslav, Greek, Czechoslovak, and French villages in World War II.

Not only do we feel overwhelming anger at the injustice of this; there is a particular irony we register at the hypocrisy that portrays our adversaries as the friends of democracy and civilization even as we loiter without term in the basements of degradation and inhuman savagery. Thus I want to say to these hypocrites, look, really look carefully at this sequence of photographs that represents the universal process of aging, perhaps more harshly imposed on us by our predicament; the process takes us from the happy potential of childhood, to the openness of cheerful adolescence, to the strong defensive awareness of being a Palestinian under siege, to the

Damascus, 1983. Sayida Zeinab camp. Girl newly arrived from Lebanon.

Bir Zeit, 1984. A student.

161

New York, 1978. A Palestinian counter-demonstrator at a pro-Israeli march.

careworn and suffering symbol of the modern casualty. If you look at this dynastic passage from youth to age, if you take it in with the eyes of someone for whom photographs are not the exhibition of a foreign specimen of some sort, you will see in it the representation of people for whom you care with concern and affection – family members or intimate friends. You will almost certainly conclude, however, that you see before you a dispiriting and sad process, as it has come to settle in an old woman's suffering face; in Yeats's words, 'a harsh reproof . . . That changed some childish day to tragedy'.

In the same poem, 'Among School Children,' Yeats brings the misfortunes of age down to the intimate uncertainties of a 'youthful mother, a shape upon her lap/ Honey of generation had betrayed.' would she think her child, 'With sixty or more winters on its head,/ A compensation for the pang of his birth,/ Or the uncertainty of his setting forth?' Surely we are entitled to ask the same question of our own history. We too are subject to time, development, change, and decline, a fact that must dispel any notion that Palestinians are a sort of essentialized paradigm of permanent homelessness and terror. We deny such a notion both politically and philosophically, in a context similar to that of Yeats's poem, where a mature consciousness investigates, confronts, and meditates on the concrete genealogy of its present self-awareness.

The knowledge and responsibility we require of ourselves and of others are those of which Yeats speaks, 'where/ The body is not bruised to pleasure soul,' where we and our history blend as do

162

Old woman in camp near Ramah, Galilee, 1979.

dancer and dance, by which we can see ourselves not as disembodied presences of Sorrow or Homelessness, but as our poets and writers see us, embodied in the fullness of our experience, as the result of our history of struggle and failure – plus something more.

For I do not think that we Palestinians are best understood, either by strangers or by ourselves, as the mathematical or photographically exact equivalent of what we have experienced. Nor are we, for non-Palestinians, for Jews and Israelis, simply the Other, some figure of foreignness and alterity that can be represented by a photograph on an identity card. Whatever the claim may be that we make on the world – and certainly on ourselves as people who have become restless in the fixed place to which we have been assigned – in fact our truest reality is expressed in the way we cross over from one place to another. We are migrants and perhaps hybrids in, but not of, any situation in which we find ourselves. This is the deepest continuity of our lives as a nation in exile and constantly on the move. We cannot always see this quality in ourselves, nor have we always wanted to, but a suggestion of this, for me at least, is an occasional possibility offered by moments

Gaza, 1979. Child labor.

Village of Senjel, near Ramallah, 1979. Rescued bird.

captured in some of Jean Mohr's photographs, in which exhilaration and energy and pleasure rise out of the ranks, so to speak, and address you forcefully, but with a graceful directness that reminds you that movement need not always be either flight or exile. In the boy's cheerfully vulnerable triumph, you can see a hint of that provisional success and momentary flair that many of us have developed in our lives: To be a Palestinian often entails mastery without domination, pleasure without injury to others.

These are fugitive qualities of our existence, to be sure. Even someone who has been elated by photographs of exuberant youngsters would nevertheless have to come back to the prevailing sadness of Palestinian life. For not only do we feel a dispiriting powerlessness about the mediocrity, violence, and human waste that do much to define our environment; we are also enveloped by a nagging disquiet at how much yet needs to be done by us. We live in a protracted not-yet, which is not always a very hopeful one. I feel it particularly as I end this book. Not yet has there been a full history of us as a people, not even a full record of what has been done to us, what outrages have been done in our name, and what we have done to others.

My own purpose here was, with Jean Mohr, to give a sense of what our essential national incompleteness is now, a sense that I believed could be rendered only from the inside, sympathetically and collaboratively. The absence of resolution in this book is a true one: It comes from exile. I had hoped in the course of writing this book to be able to take a trip to the West Bank and Gaza; some Israeli friends had promised to check the feasibility of this, and to get me

165

some assurances that I would be admitted, that I could move about safely, that I could leave when I wished. I had then planned to add a conclusion after my return. The idea was to have rounded out the photographs with the result of a direct encounter in Palestine with Palestinians, and with Israelis. But I still await conclusive news, and this uncertainty, I believe, is probably more congruent with my anomalous position, which is itself a reflection of the political ambiguities in which we are all caught.

I would like to think, though, that such a book not only tells the reader about us, but in some way also reads the reader. I would like to think that we are not just the people seen or looked at in these photographs: We are also looking at our observers. We Palestinians sometimes forget that – as in country after country, the surveillance, confinement, and study of Palestinians is part of the political process of reducing our status and preventing our national fulfillment except as the Other who is opposite and unequal, always on the defensive – we too are looking, we too are scrutinizing, assessing, judging. We are more than someone's object. We do more than stand passively in front of whoever, for whatever reason, has wanted to look at us. If you cannot finally see this about us, we will not allow ourselves to believe that the failure has been entirely ours. Not any more.

Jerusalem, 1979. The photographer photographed.

The Fall of Beirut

Contemporary Palestinian history is now strung out across the Arab world, embodied in the exile population (which today constitutes half our total number) and the places of exile–Cairo, Damascus, Amman, Kuwait, Baghdad, Tripoli, Tunis, Riyadh. But there has been no place for us like Beirut, a city of staggering violence and unpredictable resilience. Officially the Palestinian link with Lebanon was severed in late August 1982, when the PLO, led by Yasir Arafat, evacuated the city in which they had been besieged by Israeli armies for three months. Yet over 300,000 Palestinians remain, and the extraordinary drama of Beirut runs on, both for those who are still there and for those of us who left but are still tied to the place.

I never thought that Beirut was the Middle Eastern Paris, or that Lebanon was like Switzerland. This does not make the country's present agonies any less horrible, or Beirut's relentlessly detailed self-dismantling – much of it performed on prime-time television – any less unprecedented or interminably, senselessly miserable to witness. The whole process has by now become a large-scale version of the Laurel and Hardy film about two men vengefully destroying each other's car and house piece by piece, tit for tat, and while they glower and puff through many 'take thats,' the world around them gets wiped out. If the struggle for power and territory continues unchecked in Beirut, very little of either will be left when, and if, a final victor emerges. A close Palestinian friend of mine who has lived through the entire ordeal told me over the phone from Beirut that quite apart from putting up with the bombing and mayhem, reading the epidemic of local newspapers would certainly drive anyone crazy; no two of them say the same thing, and trying to figure out what is happening or who is fighting whom for what reason is like catching clouds.

Members of my immediate family still live in Beirut, as does the largest part of my wife's family, which is Lebanese. These incomprehensibly brave people are too stubborn, too unwilling to start lives over again, too anchored in the city to leave. As a Palestinian I haven't thought it prudent to visit Lebanon since 1982, although my wife, Mariam, and two young children have made a couple of visits since the Israeli invasion. My widowed mother valiantly hangs on all alone in her West Beirut house, quite sensibly focused on the problems of her health, the failures of electricity and telephone service, the difficulties of getting help, the collapsing Lebanese pound. I see her and our other relatives intermittently when they emerge for short spells in places like London and New York; they are fortunate in still having the means to travel. After 1983 or thereabouts Mariam and I stopped trying to note the changes in their faces or manners following a particularly trying 'round' (as the bouts of killing are called). In ways we can neither trace nor reconstruct, their mere survival seems miraculous. We find ourselves avoiding consideration of the inner damage they must have sustained. Most of our younger cousins, nieces, and nephews who have grown up in ten years of unremitting war tend to speak interchangeably of computer games, football scores, and massacres, and their easy way of pointing out differences between Grads, RPGs, and Katyushas is chilling; nevertheless their parents persist in giving them 'normal' lives. Ordinary, everyday vocabulary, for the most part, has hardly changed. Politics eerily is 'out there,' as are most of the militias, leaders, and rival parties, even though, of course, the war is everywhere.

Sabra, Shatila, and Bourj el-Barajneh – the ugly, sprawling Palestinian refugee camps lying just south of Beirut – have once again been besieged, bombed, and ravaged, this time by the Amal Shi'ite militia, originally armed and trained by the Palestinians. In spite of immense odds and numerous announcements of victory by Shi'ite spokesmen, Palestinian resistance to Amal continues unabated. In 1982, Sabra and Shatila were the sites of massacres by the Maronite Phalanges acting under the aegis of the Israeli army. A different season now, but the same victims.

I have almost given up trying to plot the changes and the turns, each of them denser and more complicated than the preceding ones, each of them astounding me with Lebanon's capacity for money-making, conspiracy, and both individual and mass murder. Yet the so-called traditional leaders and their variously mediocre progeny remain unchanged, as they forge and almost immediately betray alliances with each other, as well as with the Syrians, Palestinians, Iranians, Americans, Israelis, and Saudis (who seem to be bankrolling everyone). There is no one to admire or trust in this too long and too sordid spectacle of idiotic violence and limitless corruption. Even the innocent civilians who have gone on and on, with their brave routines, their ability to rebuild and restart their lives a dozen times, their courage under fire, must have secretly connived, one feels, with the leaders who have kept the war going. Otherwise, how could it have continued for such a long time?

This is Beirut, and not some deviation from a Parisian or a Swiss model. I knew the city first as a child during the early forties when we would pass from Palestine through Beirut's outskirts en route to a dreary mountain village, Dhour el Shweir, inexplicably loved by my father. Coming from or going to Palestine and Egypt were the main routes in my life then. Lebanon's mountains symbolized for me an unrelieved tedium I have experienced nowhere else. During the long mountain summers we would go to Beirut only once, except for the two passages through it into and out of the country. In the morning we visited a bank where my father changed some money; then we would spend the rest of the day at a beach where the swimming was sheer beauty.

Beirut grew tremendously during the fifties and sixties, decades when all around Lebanon revolutions and coups brought into the country a sizable number of dissident or dispossessed classes, intellectual, political, and commercial. The Palestinians constituted by far the largest and most influential of these groups. Lebanon and Palestine had always been linked through trade, connections between families, and history. It was natural that the Palestinians dispersed by the establishment of Israel would flee to Lebanon, where they were almost a whole society, not just a layer at the top of one. The intensity of these assorted influxes was very great, however, and, it now seems in retrospect, too much for Lebanon to have borne. One could see it in Beirut's physical appearance, which changed from a city constructed around a central *kasbah* with various outlying (largely ethnically and religiously composed) districts, to a city resembling nothing so much as a series of immense heaps, some very fancy, some very poor. A few districts—Ashrafiyé, for example, which remained Christian and middle to upper class— retained their substructure of sectarian identity; others simply expanded into whatever was profitable or expedient. Nightclubs, restaurants, boutiques, and banks were the preferred growth industries of this period. By the mid-seventies, West Beirut became the Palestinian quarter; Fakahany, a district bordering on the largest camps, was referred to as 'the Republic of Palestine.'

Beirut's real heyday, when it became a great world center of financial and commercial services, was the result of the oil boom, which had the effect of accelerating and exaggerating all the processes already at work in Lebanon generally, and Beirut in particular. After almost thirty years of unsatisfying transits through it, I spent my first complete year in Beirut during 1972–73, and my still vivid recollection of that year is marked by a sense of how everything seemed possible in Beirut then – every kind of person, every idea and identity, every extreme of wealth and poverty – and how the incoherence of the whole seemed to abate and even disappear in either the pleasures or the agonies of the moment, a scintillating seminar discussion or a horrendously cruel Israeli raid on South Lebanon. That year was crucial for me, in that Beirut allowed me to reeducate myself in Arabic language and literature; for twenty years I had exclusively studied the literatures of the West, whereas now I could experience the riches of my own tradition. As this was also the time of Palestinian renaissance in politics and culture, my year in Beirut, followed by a string of summers there, became a very important period for me.

One episode from those days in the early seventies provided disquieting indications of the troubles that were to come. After my father died in 1971, we planned to bury him according to his wishes in the mountain village he had loved since 1942. He was well known there and had been a benefactor of Dhour el Shweir in many ways. Most of the friends he had in Lebanon after he moved there in 1963 were men and women from the village. Yet when it came to buying a tiny bit of land in one of the local graveyards we had a grotesque time, the still angry memory of which prevents me from recounting it in detail. Suffice it to say that we were unable to conclude an agreement with any of the Christian churches in Dhour except one, and when that one accepted our offer we got so many telephoned bomb threats as to end our plan completely. I realized that my father was an outsider, a Palestinian (*ghareeb,* a stranger, was the euphemism), and no matter how jolly they were when he was alive, the residents wouldn't tolerate his long-term presence even after he had died.

This was well before 'the events' actually began in 1975, but already the number of compartments in which Lebanese life was led, and through which one passed in the course of a day, had become dizzying. Suddenly, in the mid-seventies, one realized that the compartments were there, but the corridor between them was not. Nor did they all stand on one continuous piece of ground. Beirut was transformed into a collection of overlapping territories with extensions in the Arab world, Europe, America, and Israel – extensions and interests that would easily overcome the imperfectly maintained balance within Lebanon's actual geographical boundaries. The first street barricades appeared in the summer of 1975, and I can remember the shock of fear and uncertainty I experienced one Sunday in August as I drove through East Beirut en route to Brummana, a pleasant mountain resort. There, at the end of a street I had routinely traversed over a period of weeks, was a barbed-wire-and-log obstruction, patrolled by young men brandishing automatic rifles. This was also the first time I experienced the most common of all feelings in the disintegration of

Beirut – that as a civilian, and especially a Palestinian, one was helplessly at the mercy of armed men whose guiding authority was somewhere else. You could be killed here and now, at the direction of people who were sitting in a distant Syrian palace, an American embassy, an Israeli office, or a Lebanese chalet.

A plausible theory constructed by the Lebanese sociologist Samir Khalaf has it that Ras Beirut, a promontory jutting out of West Beirut into the sea, the area where the American University is located, contained within it until the Civil War a nonsectarian, pluralistic, and open community of scholars, political activists, business people, and artists unlike anything else in the Arab world. Much of the revival of Palestinian culture and thought occurred in Ras Beirut. Khalaf is right, I think, although in the understandable anguish of his lament over Ras Beirut's passing (it is now parceled out between Druze and Shi'ite factions), he doesn't strongly enough acknowledge the latent religious or sectarian feelings that were being temporarily held at bay by consensus within Ras Beirut. But the fact is that in Ras Beirut, as in greater Beirut, everyone knew what everyone else's religion and sect and ethnic origin were. They were acknowledged almost subliminally, it is true, but they *were* noted. You registered and heard it registered that Vahé was an Armenian from Smyrna active in Maronite politics, or that Monah was a Sunni intellectual much attracted to Sartre and Abdel Nasser, or that Violette was a Palestinian Christian who had thrown her lot in with the Arab Nationalist Movement.

In my exile from it, things continue to haunt me about Beirut, and about its depressing fate as a major city. One is its marginality. While the people of this densely populated metropolis tear each other apart without much perceptible reference to any one central antagonism – also without any specifiable reason for doing so – the world looks on with considerable fascination, but little engagement. Beirut *was* a free place (for those who could afford it), it had a free press, it furnished the Arab world with the most cosmopolitan of entertainments and *loisirs*. Little of this seems to have lasted, although paradoxically Lebanese books, newspapers, and magazines are still easily the liveliest in the region.

The second thing about Beirut's unhappy fate is the insidious role played by religious and sectarian conviction. I'm ashamed to admit that a great many of my early memories of friends and family expressing religious opinions are harsh and unpleasant. 'Moslems,' I was told in 1954 by a great friend of my father's, 'are dust. They should be blown away.' Another good Christian, a prominent philosopher and former Lebanese foreign minister, frequently denounced Islam and the Prophet Mohammed to me, using such words as 'lechery,' 'hypocrisy,' 'corruption,' and 'degeneration.' These, I later discovered, were not isolated opinions. As anyone who has followed the discourse of Christian militancy in Lebanon and elsewhere in the region will know, they have come to constitute the core of minority expression, which in turn furnished the majority Muslim community with a permanent provocation. Such compliments tend to be, and have obviously been, reciprocated. The result is consolidated animosity, what William Hazlitt calls 'the pleasure of hating.' A feature of this pleasure, Hazlitt said, is that it 'eats into the heart of religion, and turns it into rankling spleen and bigotry; it makes patriotism an excuse for carrying fire, pestilence, and famine into other lands: it leaves to virtue nothing but the spirit of censoriousness, and a narrow, jealous, inquisitorial watchfulness over the actions and motives of others.' The relevance of these words to that nasty mix of religious zeal and nationalism sweeping through Lebanon, Israel, and Iran – and the United States, which has a history of involvement in all three countries – is perfectly evident.

There is no denying the terrible sadness and anger one feels about Beirut's ruination. I'm certain both are evident in what I've written here. I can't fully grasp what Beirut's citizens must be going through (although Mariam occasionally gives me glimpses of a sorrow that is very deep indeed), but I can in a general way venture a response on behalf of exiles like myself – Palestinians for whom Beirut provided a substitute home. However much we go on about Lebanese corruption and superficiality and violence, we feel ourselves now to be sadly out in the cold. Beirut's genius was that it responded immediately to our needs as Arabs in an Arab world already gone repressive, drab, and insufferably mediocre. For some years one could, in Beirut, burn with a hard, gemlike flame; even the city's vice and profligacy had a brilliance you could not see elsewhere. The only thing contemporary Beirut did not give us was staying power, or enough feelings of concern for the rather fragile foundations that its dazzling hospitality covered. The main consolation of these dark times is the sentiment that since Beirut once rose from obscurity it might again reappear from out of its catastrophic destruction, and with it a solider, more caring citizenry. For Palestinians – and for Arabs and Israelis generally – the benefits in increased tolerance and community would be certain.

⦙⦙⦙⦙⦙⦙⦙⦙⦙⦙⦙